Praise
The CEO and the BOARD

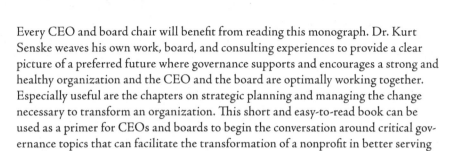

Every CEO and board chair will benefit from reading this monograph. Dr. Kurt Senske weaves his own work, board, and consulting experiences to provide a clear picture of a preferred future where governance supports and encourages a strong and healthy organization and the CEO and the board are optimally working together. Especially useful are the chapters on strategic planning and managing the change necessary to transform an organization. This short and easy-to-read book can be used as a primer for CEOs and boards to begin the conversation around critical governance topics that can facilitate the transformation of a nonprofit in better serving the Church and the world.

—BART DAY, MDIV, MBA; PRESIDENT AND CEO,
LUTHERAN CHURCH EXTENSION FUND

Dr. Senske's book provides a comprehensive review of governance best practices from noted governance experts. He goes on to encourage you to practically apply the principles learned to your own organization because you know what your organization needs better than anyone else.

—TERESA RASMUSSEN, PRESIDENT AND CEO, THRIVENT

The timing of Dr. Senske's book is impeccable. With the rapidly changing landscape facing most organizations, CEOs and boards must work in tandem to leverage the things that strengthen performance and maintain absolute clarity about why this work is critical for the betterment of our communities. Senske's experiences and insights enable readers to create a road map leading toward a positive future for their organization. The reflective questions included in this book are great starting points for conversation and reflection.

—LINDA TIMMONS, PRESIDENT AND CEO, MOSAIC

Dr. Senske recognizes the tough challenges facing CEOs and boards in today's increasingly complex and ever-changing environment. He offers powerful insights and practical advice on both the art and science of governance. This is a must-read for nonprofit CEOs and boards that want a strategic board of directors to create a competitive advantage and achieve their organization's potential.

—CHARLOTTE HABERAECKER, PRESIDENT AND CEO,
LUTHERAN SERVICES IN AMERICA

A breath of fresh air! This is not your ordinary one-size-fits-all governance prescription, but a thoughtful conversation on the intricacies of modern-day governance and the centrality of the board and CEO relationship. Applying his own deep experience, Dr. Senske artfully navigates the subtle and not-so-subtle challenges and barriers to organizational success at the governance level. Rather than providing trite solutions, Senske encourages the reader with new perspectives and opportunities for deeper thought designed to help the reader find the right path for their own unique organization. Well worth reading!

—Kurt Buchholz, president and CEO, Lutheran Hour Ministries

Dr. Senske's rich and provocative insights into nonprofit governance best practices is a must-read for board chairs, members, and CEOs. This book moves at a fast, satisfying pace and provides scores of questions and topics that help heighten the individual and collective self-awareness of board members. Good stewardship suggests that every board and CEO collaboratively read and explore Senske's work as part of a self-evaluation and improvement initiative. Repeating this process every few years and using the book as a reference when governance issues and opportunities arise will help us lead our nonprofits to outcomes that best serve our communities. They deserve nothing less.

—Don Scifres, founder and managing director, 28:20 Capital

The most important aspect of governance expert Dr. Kurt Senske's insightful book is that he recognizes upfront that nonprofit organizations do in fact operate in highly competitive arenas. Yes, they are vital service organizations, but they must compete for constituent attention, gifted leaders, engaged experts, and financial resources. And what Senske makes clear is that the right governance structure and board composition can make the difference between mediocrity and excellence in those competitive endeavors.

—Kirk D. Farney, PhD, vice president for advancement, vocation, and alumni engagement, Wheaton College, Wheaton, Illinois

As nonprofit leaders, we desire to be good stewards of the organizations entrusted to our care. Dr. Senske challenges us to unleash the often hidden power of the CEO-board relationship! As a nonprofit CEO for fifteen years, I was affirmed by this book for many things I have learned on my journey. Senske's book also provided clarity and focus in many other areas. Dr. Senske challenged me as a nonprofit leader to refocus my thoughts and efforts to gain a real competitive advantage for my organization. This is a must-read for nonprofit CEOs, boards, and leaders at all levels!

—James Sanft, president and CEO, Concordia Plan Services

For the better part of four decades, I have been connected to voluntary boards—both on the staff side and the officer side. Over the years, my work with small, local congregations, community organizations, higher education institutions, and multimillion-dollar international nonprofits would have benefited from this book. Dr. Senske is a guru and a guide when it comes to governance. A favorite feature for me is the book's probing and practical questions. Raising the right questions raises effectiveness, or as Paul puts it, "Whatever . . . is commendable . . . think about these things" (Philippians 4:8).

—REV. JOHN ARTHUR NUNES, PhD;
PASTOR, PILGRIM LUTHERAN CHURCH, SANTA MONICA, CALIFORNIA;
SENIOR FELLOW, CENTER FOR RELIGION, CULTURE, AND DEMOCRACY

Dr. Senske's years of acumen, insight, and skill in the boardroom—both as CEO and as a board member—give him a unique vantage point to study what works and what doesn't. This is a great book for board directors and executives alike. You will find yourself nodding along and discovering new insights that will help you navigate with success.

—MANDY TUONG, PRESIDENT AND CEO,
THRIVENT CHARITABLE IMPACT AND INVESTING

This is a book for which nonprofit CEOs and boards have been waiting. Dr. Senske's work is exceedingly relevant to the real opportunities and challenges nonprofit organizations face today. His focus on the art and science of leadership and boardsmanship is balanced, clearly stated, and effectively nuanced. The book is immensely practical. There is no pie-in-the-sky, magic-wand thinking herein. Dr. Senske's real-life examples are illustrative but also timely, useful, and practical. This book goes far beyond being a how-to manual. It is, more importantly, a why-to and what-to resource for CEOs and boards who aspire to excellence, ongoing growth, and fulfillment of their organizations' missions and visions.

—BRIAN FRIEDRICH, BA '79, MDIV, PhD,
PRESIDENT, CONCORDIA UNIVERSITY, ST. PAUL

The CEO
and
the BOARD

The Art of Nonprofit Governance
as a Competitive Advantage

KURT SENSKE

CONCORDIA PUBLISHING HOUSE · SAINT LOUIS

I am profoundly grateful for the love
and support of my wife, Laurie;
father and sainted mother, Al and Ruth;
daughter and son-in-law, Sydney and Cody.
Thank you for making me a better person.

This book is dedicated to you, the reader,
who, through your leadership roles
in organizations, strive to make our
communities and world a better place.

Published by Concordia Publishing House
3558 S. Jefferson Avenue, St. Louis, MO 63118-3968
1-800-325-3040 • cph.org

Manufactured in the United States of America

1   2   3   4   5   6   7   8   9   10   32   31   30   29   28   27   26   25   24   23

Table of Contents

Introduction

As CEOs and board members, we lead in an environment that is experiencing an accelerated rate of change. The world in which we operate is increasingly uncertain, complex, and competitive. How an organization utilizes technology is now directly related to its ability to remain relevant and competitive. We are rightfully tasked with weaving the values of openness, integrity, diversity, trust, empowerment, employee development, and learning into the daily fabric of our organizational culture.

Funding streams have become less certain. Employees are empowered to share unfiltered opinions of their employer and/or CEO on websites for all to see. Virtually every organization is being asked whether it is having a positive environmental impact. In many realms, stakeholders are now demanding evidence-based, or at least, evidence-informed outcomes. Leaders are expected to be available 24/7 and board members increasingly find it difficult to devote the necessary time to their board service. As I write, we leaders are being asked to simultaneously navigate COVID-19 complexities, supply-chain issues, a dearth of available employees, a potential world war, and inflationary pressures. Organizational complexity, the permeation of technology throughout all aspects of the organization, increased scrutiny, and sociocultural shifts have made the roles of both the CEO and the board more difficult. No matter what type of organization you lead, leadership is not for the faint of heart.

Unfortunately, our existing board-governance models are not well suited for this new normal. Articles of incorporation and bylaws that may have been well designed when originally crafted have now become a hindrance to organizational success. A board's current culture may have been appropriate for the past but not the future. Founding CEOs or long-tenured board members may wield an inordinate amount of influence, stifling creativity. Skill sets, personalities, and experiences necessary for an effective CEO and board member a decade ago may not be a good fit for today. Board members often lack a shared understanding of what their role is.

For board members and organizational leaders who govern in this new normal, the question becomes how does an organization adapt its governance model so that it adds real, measurable value to its mission? so that it becomes a competitive advantage? The time has come for the board and CEO to view board governance as a nonnegotiable organizational differentiator. This intentional focus will add value to your mission and bottom line as you adapt your organization to a myriad of changes, both external and internal. With intentionality, a board and senior leadership can collectively work together to implement an evolving, adaptive model of governance that is tailored to the current situation of your unique organization.

No two organizations are alike, so the purpose of this book is to provide a roadmap that will allow CEOs and their boards to openly examine and adapt their governance model to be designed to drive organizational missional success. Those organizations and their members who embark down this path will be at a competitive advantage vis-à-vis their peers who do not. This is the art of governance.

CHAPTER 1

Why Should You Listen to Me?

To assess whether this approach may add value to your organization, allow me to briefly describe my experience as it relates to board governance. During my career, I have viewed this governance dance from the perspective of a CEO, board member, and consultant. I have been privileged to serve on eleven different boards of directors, including as chair of the boards of a Fortune 500 financial services company, an international relief agency, an $800 million charitable foundation, and a global missions organization with offices in thirty-six countries. I have served as a member of the boards of a national trade association, the national denomination of my church body, a homeowner's association, a statewide alliance of children's services providers, a very small startup 501(c)(3) organization, and a local private school. I have led or participated in six CEO searches (five of which we got right) and have served on countless investment, governance, audit, finance, risk, and personnel committees.

During my 600-plus board meetings, collectively we have made decisions as mundane as which staff should be entrusted with the keys to the school kitchen and as significant as approving a merger between two Fortune 500 companies. I also participated in a controversial, albeit correct, decision (in my opinion) to close a small private university. I have served on both healthy and dysfunctional boards of directors and have participated in the governance of thriving as well as less-than-successful organizations.

I have worked with outstanding and mediocre CEOs and have experienced narcissistic as well as truly humble Level 5[1] servant leaders. During my board service, we have hired what proved to be outstanding CEOs and have helped others find a more suitable vocation. There have been times as board chair that I have had to counsel board members that their talents might be better used elsewhere. I have observed board members work, scream, laugh, cry, and pray together.

I have also survived and thrived on the other side of the ledger. For twenty-three years, I had the privilege of serving as CEO of a large, multi-state, social service/education organization with over $100 million in annual revenue and just over one thousand employees. During my tenure, I reported to seven different board chairs and countless board members, each with unique personalities, varying skill sets, and different governing philosophies. Despite our differences and occasional friction, collectively we worked together to quadruple the size of the organization and significantly enhance its societal impact while at the same time strengthening its balance sheet to ensure future stability. We continually adjusted our governance model to reflect the always-changing external and internal realities, appropriately understanding that governance is as much an art as it is a science.

I enjoyed a close working relationship with my board, albeit there were a few brief moments in history when one or two individual board members felt like more of a hindrance than a true partner. I say this in recognition of my own shortcomings and to acknowledge that on this side of heaven, no CEO-board relationship will ever be perfect.

Wearing the hat of a consultant to boards and CEOs provides yet another perspective. I have advised numerous other boards and CEOs, who, in most cases, knew that their governance process needed improvement and wisely chose a third party to help address the proverbial elephant(s) in the room. Often it is easier for an outsider, who has no stake other than to add value to an organization, to facilitate a conversation around sensitive topics about the obstacles—structural, external, or internal—that are preventing the organization from achieving its full potential.

The purpose of this book is not to take the side of either the CEO or a board member. Having served in virtually all capacities, I no longer think of the board-staff relationship in terms of "us versus them." Rather, we are all on the same team. For this approach to succeed, this relationship simply must be a shared partnership. Governance as a potential competitive advantage must be acknowledged and endorsed by both the CEO and the board, knowing that each role is vital if the organization is to achieve its goal of utilizing its board governance to achieve organizational gain.

To protect the privacy of individuals and the confidentiality of the various organizations, a few details have been slightly altered to ensure anonymity. Any identifying resemblance to actual individuals and organizations is merely coincidental. For purposes of brevity, I use the term *CEO* to refer to the organization leader, knowing that the reader who reports to a board may have the title of Chief Executive Officer, Executive Director, Superintendent, Commissioner, General Manager, Principal, President, or Senior Pastor. As this is a team sport, I also believe that there is value in educating the senior leadership team of an organization in the art of governance. In many organizations, members of the senior leadership team play an active role in boardrooms and are increasingly an integral aspect of effective board governance.

CHAPTER 2

Boards and CEOs Simply Must Adapt

As I reflect on my career, I am struck by how dramatically the external environment in which CEOs and boards operate has changed. The complexity of the enterprise, heightened competition, tighter margins, the impact of technology, increasing and appropriate emphasis on diversity, changing ethical standards, and increased awareness of organizations' environmental impacts have all made the roles of both CEOs and board members much more complex than even five years ago.

Very few CEOs or board members have the background to truly understand their organization's information technology strategy and accompanying risks. Millennials have different work expectations than Gen Xers or Boomers. Strategies to appeal to the generational segmentation of an organization's donors have become necessarily multilayered, time-consuming, and expensive. Social media, internet-accessible details of CEO compensation packages, and websites such as Glass Door—which gathers employee-generated feedback on both organizations and their CEOs—make living in a fishbowl a daily reality for CEOs and boards of organizations of all sizes. One misstep, whether intentional or not, can destroy reputations, organizations, and careers.

The distinction between nonprofit and for-profit organizations is also becoming blurred. Nonprofit organizations are increasingly competing with for-profit companies in industries such as social services, health care, and education. Charter schools are blurring the distinction between public and private schools. Nonprofit organizations are establishing for-profit subsidiaries to create additional funding streams. To recruit and retain Millenials and Gen Z, for-profit companies are increasingly touting their missional reach. Benchmarks such as community and environmental impact are now just as likely to be part of an executive's incentive plan in a publicly traded company as is maximizing shareholder value.

Boards of large nonprofit organizations and universities are increasingly looking for leaders with complex for-profit organizational experience as a nonnegotiable skill set and are being forced to provide market-appropriate compensation packages to acquire such talent. In some organizations, the skill set of the CEO may be superior to that of the board members. These external changes often require a different set of talents and time commitment at the board level that many boards simply haven't recognized, or if they have, are scrambling to catch up, with varying degrees of success.

The distinctions in governance models between the various corporate structures are also becoming blurred. Nonprofit and family-held organizations increasingly have designed their board-governance models to mimic the best practices of Fortune 500 companies—sometimes referred to as the Sarbanes-Oxley Act, named after the congressional legislation that governs publicly traded companies.[2] Others have implemented governance models created specifically for nonprofit organizations; these include the Carver model, coined after nonprofit governance guru John Carver.[3] Still others have developed a hybrid of the two. Alternatively, for-profit companies are increasingly looking at mission-focused organizations for guidance as they recognize the responsibilities they have to their employees, environment, and communities in which they operate.

In my experience, it is often the nonprofit organizations, family-owned companies, universities, church-affiliated organizations, and foundations that suffer from a lack of rigorous governance practices. Some, for example, continue to populate their boards with *friends and family* or those who are well-meaning but lack the necessary experience. Others ignore term limits as a best practice. They have failed to learn from their publicly traded counterparts who have been forced in recent years by shareholders, social-purpose investors, class-action attorneys, and regulatory bodies to take organizational governance seriously. In what I believe is a promising sign, CEOs and board members from the for-profit world are increasingly bringing their governance best practices with them to the table as they volunteer their time with nonprofit organizations.

No two organizations are alike. A private university has its own unique governance needs, as does a charter school or health-care organization. The same governance model may not be appropriate for a trade association and a foundation. The highly regulated, multi-state, 136-year-old organization that I served as CEO has much different governance needs than the 501(c)(3) startup nonprofit organization complete with one part-time employee that several of us recently created. No matter what type of organization you play a leadership role in, and as important as selecting an appropriate governance model is, this is only one piece of the solution. It is simply no longer enough for boards and CEOs to merely implement one of the many readily available conceptual frameworks as they attempt, often in vain, to fulfill their governance responsibilities.

CHAPTER 3

The Issue

During my leadership journey, I have spent countless hours listening to scores of frustrated CEOs and board members. All desire to make a positive impact on their organization. And while most can point to certain degrees of success, deep in their hearts, they know that they don't yet have it quite right. Boards and CEOs engage in an awkward dance as they search in vain for an effective partnership or a new model of governance. During this unsatisfying journey, some board members quit in frustration, and, on occasion, a CEO prematurely leaves, voluntarily or otherwise.

In the United States, there are currently more than 1.5 million nonprofit organizations and approximately 2,600 universities and colleges. In addition, there are also more than 4 million privately held companies and more than 300,000 churches. All of them are of varying sizes, differing histories, unique missions, and varying leadership skill sets and sophistication. Some have a strong balance sheet, while others struggle to make payroll. Many are new, while others are more than 100 years old. Some are still led by their founders, while others have had to reinvent themselves to remain relevant.

Contrary to the advice of some consultants, there will never be one uniform governance model that a board and CEO can get trained in and adopt. It may be the starting point, but it is never the end. Yes, there are basic building blocks of governance that every board member needs to be cognizant of and adhere to. However, it is also true that every organization is necessarily unique, each with distinct, evolving governance needs. To assume that it makes sense for each organization to implement a uniform governance model simply flies in the face of reality.

Maybe the closest analogy is that of a large family. While you know there are parenting books to help and minimum standards of behavior that are expected so the state doesn't take your child away, as a parent, you also intuitively know each child is unique and that different parenting skills, rules, and boundaries must be utilized to be effective. The carrots and sticks that are appropriate for a two-year-old may not be appropriate for an eighteen-year-old. As a child becomes a young adult, the relationship may become almost one of peers, knowing that each retains its own separate set of responsibilities and activities. A family that is spread throughout the country or world is going to have different communication needs than a family that lives together in the same community. Families who are unable to pay their bills will have different conversations than those who can.

Similarly, each organization and its governance structure, by definition, is unique. The board of an organization that is having difficulty meeting its bond covenants is going to need to dig deeper into the data and possibly meet more often than the board of an organization that is seemingly firing on all cylinders. A board with a new CEO will want to spend extra time building a relationship, finding agreement on the organization's mission and strategy going forward, and establishing the appropriate metrics to measure success. A board embarking on a new-CEO search will obviously need to devote additional time to fulfill its responsibilities. A potential merger opportunity will require more of the board's attention. Deciding if it is in your organization's interest to change your brand or more narrowly tailor your mission will require a different level of board involvement. Negative media attention or a less-than-ethical action by the CEO will lead to at least a temporary change in the dynamic of the governance model.

Every organization goes through different seasons in its life. During my twenty-three years as CEO, I have seen the pendulum swing from worrying about making bond covenants as a result of the simultaneous impact of a major hurricane and recession, to becoming debt free with an endowment of over $40 million. How we spend the earnings of the endowment requires a different type of involvement from the board than trying to please your investment bankers during difficult financial times. Going through a rebranding process and repositioning our mission took an entirely different level of board involvement than working with them to tweak our now very focused mission after several years of successful implementation. Making difficult decisions to close or sell programs due to external changes in the environment demanded a temporary modification of our board governance process to ensure that staff and board continued to walk in lockstep and that good decisions were made.

It is the responsibility of every board and CEO to intentionally and continuously re-create the right governance model that is effective in its unique situation. For this to be successful, the board and CEO collectively will need to clarify their respective roles, engage in a robust conversation regarding the current needs of their organization, have an open dialogue about the elephants in the room, honestly assess the totality of their collective skill sets, and intentionally strengthen the board-CEO partnership.

CHAPTER 4

An Exercise in Frustration

Even though it has been empirically demonstrated that effective corporate governance is a key predictor of organizational success,[4] many boards fail in this shared responsibility. As a CEO, if you are completely honest, you will acknowledge that there are times when your board is not performing to its full potential. Board members miss meetings, appear to be unengaged, or are not as generous in their donations as their financial situation would seem to indicate. On the other side of the coin, board members who signed up to make a difference often feel powerless or become frustrated when their wisdom is seemingly ignored. A lack of trust emerges, resulting in either an overreaction or a loss of passion for the mission of the organization.

I have witnessed situations where, simultaneously, the board doesn't feel empowered and the CEO believes he is being micromanaged. The laundry list of concerns is endless. Board members fret that the organization isn't achieving its goals. The CEO perceives that the board doesn't have the requisite skill sets to be of value. The board doesn't believe it is receiving the right information. The staff doesn't have confidence that the board can effectively lead a CEO-search process. Board members quietly wonder why the CEO is paid so much. The CEO notices that the board rarely compliments her work or acknowledges her sacrifices. Board members feel controlled by the CEO and wonder who is managing whom. New board members often discover that the existing board members have become a rubber stamp, don't understand the business, or have not established processes to effectively evaluate the CEO and/or organization. The list goes on. For these and a host of other reasons, both boards and CEOs are often left unsatisfied with their organizations' current governance model.

This is not a new dilemma. Humorist Mark Twain famously commented, "In the first place God made idiots. This was for practice. Then He made School Boards."[5] More seriously, management guru Peter Drucker observed that the inability to function is the one issue that all boards have in common.[6] Board consultants John and Miriam Carver add, "Board members are usually intelligent and experienced persons as individuals. Yet boards, as groups, are mediocre. . . . Boards tend to be, in fact, incompetent groups of competent individuals."[7]

There have been a host of excellent resources written on governance to assist boards and CEOs in enhancing their governance model. Tomes that have stood the test of time include Richard Chait, Barbara Taylor, and William Ryan's *Governance as Leadership*;[8] Colin Carter and Jay Lorsch's *Back to the Drawing Board*;[9] and John Carver's *Boards That Make a Difference*.[10] Every leader and board member would be wise to absorb and learn from their wisdom.

There are also numerous organizations with the primary mission of promoting better organizational governance. They include the National Association of Corporate Directors, BoardSource, the Association of Governing Boards of Universities and Colleges, and the National Association of Board of Directors. Search the internet for *"best practices board governance,"* and you will be overwhelmed with close to five million results providing usually free and mostly sound counsel. Whether you are looking for a conflict-of-interest form, investment committee charter, or CEO evaluation form, it is available for download.

Despite the abundance of information available at our fingertips, something is clearly amiss. The question becomes, Where is the disconnect between the CEO, the board, good governance, and organizational success? How do you fix it? Is it even possible to fix? With everything else on your plate, why should you even care?

CHAPTER 5

Board Governance as a Competitive Advantage

In my experience, organizations that create a healthy board-CEO relationship coupled with an effective board-governance structure will enjoy a competitive advantage vis-à-vis their peers. These organizations will be more strategic and better positioned to make difficult decisions, will be able to pivot faster when necessary, and will be more competitive at attracting top talent at the senior leadership and board levels.

Harnessing this competitive advantage begins with understanding your organization. This includes acknowledging the strengths and weaknesses of your current governance model, including your legal structure. It means creating a safe environment to identify and address the proverbial elephants in the room.

- Do we have the right skill sets and appropriate diversity of experiences?

- Is the changing external environment placing our organization at risk?

- Has the process of how we select board members become a competitive disadvantage?

- Are our bylaws outdated? Have they inadvertently become a competitive disadvantage?

- Does our culture or board agenda prevent the board and CEO from engaging in challenging strategic conversations?

Many of the obstacles that limit the potential of boards and leaders to successfully lead their organizations into the future are rooted in an organization's structure, history, culture, and on occasion, simply bad habits. The first step in addressing these obstacles is for board members and CEOs to intentionally create an environment that allows for an honest conversation as together they unpeel and analyze the various layers of their unique organization.

Organizational elephants come in all shapes and sizes. My experience has been that virtually every organization has one or more elephants in the room that are currently being ignored. Elephants may include the impact of the changing external landscape, a board that doesn't have the right collective skill sets to fulfill its role, a board member or members who are poisoning the culture of the board, an organizational strategy that is no longer focused or effective, revenue streams or a customer base that is rapidly shrinking, an outdated technology strategy, a cumbersome governance model, or a legal structure that is rooted in the past. For governance to indeed be a competitive advantage as opposed to a disadvantage, one—if not the most important—role of the board and CEO is to collectively identify and address their organization's current unique elephants in the room.

This review requires courage, trust, and honesty. It will demand that both the CEO and the board members leave their egos at the door. This exercise, I would argue, is also nonnegotiable. If you as a board and CEO ignore your unique elephant, you are not fulfilling your fiduciary responsibilities as leaders of your organization.

CHAPTER 6

What Is Your Organization's Elephant in the Room?

As one example of a potential elephant, every organization must intentionally evaluate whether its legal structure is appropriate for its current competitive environment. For some organizations, this will be an easy assessment, and they will quickly move on. For others, a close examination may lead to the conclusion that their current legal structure has become a hindrance that places them at a competitive disadvantage.

For example, one organization historically selected its board members via a vote of five hundred of its members at an annual convention. While in theory, the democratic aspect of this process appealed to some, in reality, the process was less than ideal. At one convention, the members did not elect any board members with financial expertise. The reason, as far as I could surmise, was that each candidate was provided an opportunity to give a speech to the members prior to voting. The candidates with accounting and actuarial backgrounds were not as adroit in making persuasive speeches and, as a result, did not get elected. Ultimately, the bylaws were amended to allow the board of directors to select its own board members.

Another board oversees an international organization with a long history of impactful service. When the organization was founded over a century ago, its membership was limited only to men. While the bylaws and articles have, for the most part, been updated, one historical anomaly remained. The bylaws mandated that only a male can serve as chair of the board. With most of the organization's donors currently female, this had become an embarrassing historical artifact that its membership voted to change.

In yet another situation, a potential partnership with an American-based Catholic hospital got derailed because their bylaws required them to first obtain permission in a cumbersome, time-consuming process from a bureaucrat based in Rome. The point is that as an organization evolves, its current legal structure may also necessarily need to change for the organization to remain viable, nimble, and impactful. Changing the legal structure means changing its articles and bylaws that govern how it legally relates to a parent organization, foundation, or partner.

Another organization experienced a time when a majority of the members of the board simply did not trust either their colleagues or the CEO. In a futile attempt to control the various board committees as well as the CEO, the majority block created an overly prescriptive, 200-plus-page policy manual that attempted to spell out exactly how each anticipated situation should be handled. Fortunately, as new board members were elected, they quickly realized that this punitive governance model was frustrating the CEO's ability to lead and preventing their organization from achieving its potential. A board committee, including the CEO, was established to rework their board policy manual, this time from a place of mutual trust.

As you assess the appropriateness of your organization's governance structure, here are some questions you may wish to include:

- **Does the legal structure allow for the board, working with the CEO, to identify and select a qualified board with a diverse set of skills?**

- **Is the board truly empowered to make the necessary decisions? or is it beholden to a parent or partner organization?**

- **Is the CEO provided with the requisite authority to nimbly lead the organization without having to always ask the board and/or board committees for permission?**

- **Is the number of required board members appropriate? too few? too many?**

+ From a structural perspective, what is hindering the board and/or CEO from efficiently being able to lead and adjust to the changing environment?

+ Are the articles of incorporation or bylaws outdated, inefficient, or at a competitive disadvantage?

CHAPTER 7

Good Governance Is Both an Art and a Science

One hallmark of virtually every successful organization is a qualified, well-informed, passionate, and engaged board working with the right CEO and operating within an effective governance system. Both among the members of the board as well as between the board and CEO there exists a relationship built on respect, candor, and integrity. The good news is that all of this is possible if the board and CEO, working together as a team, focus their attention on both the science and art of good governance.

The *science* is the agreed-upon governance framework, the established written rules that allow the CEO and the board to manage and lead the organization. It is what is commonly known as *best practices*. These are the foundational building blocks for any organization and are vital for a board and CEO to succeed. They are mandatory and, if done properly, require knowledge of best board practices and attention to detail. As the internal and external environment evolves, what may have been an appropriate governance practice five years ago may no longer be a best practice today. If an organization exhibits a healthy governance culture, the science of governance will always continue to evolve. Every board member should be knowledgeable of and attuned to the *science* aspect of board-CEO governance. This is a necessary component of new board member orientation and continuing education. Each director should have a clear understanding of her fiduciary responsibility, often defined as duty of care, duty of loyalty, and duty of obedience.

Within this framework of the science of governance, every board has a fiduciary responsibility of oversight. Well-known examples include the fiduciary roles played by committees such as audit, investment and finance, personnel, and governance. Included in the board's responsibility to ensure there is an effective governance model in place is typically the following:

- Protect the organization's assets in all their forms: physical, intellectual, and reputational.

- Provide clarity (preferably written) as to what the board's responsibility is and what is delegated to the CEO.

- Conduct an annual audit.

- Ensure that an appropriately skilled and representative board is in place.

- Create an effective committee system with appropriate charters.

- Engage in continual succession planning.

- Provide oversight of a consistent CEO review process and some level of oversight or approval of C-suite[11] compensation, travel expenses, and contracts.

- Engage in an annual deep dive into the organization's strategy.

- Conduct a regular evaluation of the effectiveness of the board.

BoardSource, the influential nonprofit organization whose mission is to support excellence in nonprofit governance, provides eight essential practices, sixteen leading practices, and five compliance practices they recommend all boards adhere to.[12] This is the science of board governance. Every board should periodically review this type of list to determine if it is fulfilling its legal responsibilities for its unique organization.

The science of board governance is a given for effective board oversight. What most boards fail to realize is that although these best practices are the nonnegotiable starting point, they are never the end. Best practices by themselves are insufficient to support the organization in its relentless pursuit to clearly define its mission and maximize value. Board governance is not a math equation to be solved. Rather, board governance is a complex, group-dynamic, systems phenomenon not unlike the messiness of the dynamics within many of our extended families.

No one governance template, no matter how well designed, will perfectly fit the governance needs of your unique organization. Governance models such as Sarbanes-Oxley or the Carver model are excellent starting points but never, in my experience, the end game. Board members often become confused when a well-meaning board consultant announces, for example, that the board is responsible for the mission and that staff is responsible for implementation. Or asks a board to distinguish between *means* and *ends* or *outputs* versus *outcomes*. This simply doesn't compute in the real, messy world of the life of an organization. It also often leads to dedicated board members wondering what they are doing wrong and CEOs becoming exhausted in frustration.

Every organization has a unique history, personality, regulatory constraints, operating environment, strengths, weaknesses, opportunities, threats, and culture. Governing a highly regulated state- and federal-funded social-service organization will be much different than governing a foundation or international mission organization. The uniqueness of your organization will necessarily impact what board governance strategy will best drive organizational success at each specific point in time in your organization's history. Wrestling with the science of good governance is an ongoing journey that shouldn't be ignored. However, it alone will not get an organization to the holy grail of utilizing your governance model as a competitive advantage.

CHAPTER 8

The Art of Governance

What often gets left out of the equation is the *art* of the CEO-board relationship as it connects to effective board governance. The art of governance will never be neat or proceed in a straight line, as it includes such squishy niceties as emotional intelligence, leadership, character, trust, vulnerability, integrity, and passion. It takes a real commitment from all parties to make it work. Like any good marriage, the art of good governance requires humility, servanthood, humor, honesty, and forgiveness.

The art of governance is the application of the creative skills of the board members and CEO and also their creative skills, diverse experiences, imagination, and emotional intelligence as they lead and govern their organization. What is exciting about this approach is that it allows both the CEO and the board to become artists as they design and implement a leadership model that makes the most sense for their unique organization. No longer will an organization exclusively rely on a predesigned model. Rather, we can now embrace the reality that leadership is the art of the possible. As leaders, we should learn from other organizations and consultants but never copy them. The best leaders intuitively understand that they must design their own unique path to achieve their organization's mission.

Leadership in this scenario becomes the art of the possible. Unique organizational, cultural, religious, and historical nuances can now be accounted for. Every organization, within the boundaries of the science of good governance, can chart its desired destination with its unique roadmap. By embracing the art of governance, the CEO, the leadership team, and the board possess a shared responsibility to collectively design and implement a governance system that takes advantage of the uniqueness of their organization.

The art of governance, at its core, is not necessarily all that complicated. It does, however, require trust, transparency, and a shared commitment from the CEO and the board. It also requires, on occasion, difficult conversations and decisions that have real-life consequences for clients, employees, customers, the board, and occasionally the CEO. Confronting the elephants in the room—the organization's brutal facts—is nonnegotiable if an organization is to thrive.

Executing the art of governance well requires an abundance of emotional intelligence among the members of the board and leadership team. Emotional intelligence, maturity, and integrity in their individual, collective, and organizational forms, coupled with a passion for the organization's mission, are the nonnegotiable attributes needed to ensure that board governance becomes a competitive advantage. In simple terms, emotional intelligence can be defined as the ability to connect with others. It is the skill one possesses in perceiving, understanding, and managing one's emotions that then allows a leader to effectively influence those around him.

Daniel Goleman, in his pathbreaking book *Emotional Intelligence: Why It Can Matter More Than IQ*,[13] studied best-in-class performers at the renowned scientific think tank Bell Laboratories. Goleman found that the difference between the stars and other performers was not their academic IQ but their emotional IQ. They simply had a greater ability to motivate themselves and work their informal networks to drive results. When an emergency arose or a problem needed to be solved, a star performer, or star CEO who possessed a high degree of emotional intelligence, was more likely to solve the problem because she had already developed close relationships with people whose services might be needed.[14] Similarly, at a board level, its collective emotional intelligence is a, if not the, key driver to developing social harmony and effectiveness. Increasingly, as Goleman notes, as organizations (and board governance) become more complex, the fundamentals of emotional intelligence will become even more important as the board and CEO simply must cooperatively learn and work together.[15]

Emotional maturity, a cousin of emotional intelligence, is present when a leader effectively controls her reaction, handles criticism well, and creates space between feeling and appropriately reacting. A leader with emotional maturity tends to possess great empathy and thus can identify and relate to the emotions of others. This type of leader naturally holds himself accountable and possesses a unique degree of flexibility and the ability to compromise when appropriate. Boards of directors are increasingly insisting that CEOs possess both emotional intelligence and emotional maturity and are evaluating candidates on these attributes through diagnostic testing and via various interview techniques during the interview process. Executive search firms such as Spencer Stuart and Korn Ferry have gathered a body of data that indicates that without these attributes, a CEO is simply less likely to be successful.[16]

The art of governance assumes that the CEO and the board possess the appropriate soft and hard skill sets to lead as they chart their organization's unique destiny. In my experience, most, but not all, boards and CEOs, while never perfect, do possess the requisite skill sets to work well together. However, if you conclude that for one reason or the other your organization does not, it is imperative, as fiduciaries of your organization, to wrestle with and make the necessary changes. This may include selecting a different board chair. It may mean adding new board members who possess the requisite hard and soft skills. On occasion, it may also require a board to engage in a difficult conversation regarding the future of their CEO.

As a board and CEO wrestle with the art of governance, at its core, there are five primary questions to be addressed to ensure that the organization is well positioned for its governance model to become a competitive advantage:

- **Does the current legal structure continue to make sense? Or is it a hindrance to the organization's competitiveness?**

- **What processes, policies, board size, and committee structure are needed to allow the board to effectively monitor the organization as well as assess its performance?** *↖ softbiuty*

- **What individual and collective set of skills, talents, and other attributes should the board seek to ensure that they add value to the organization?**

- **How will the board define and oversee its relationship with the CEO?**

- **How will the board and CEO work together on mission and strategy?**

The goal is to effectively create a culture of governance that provides effective oversight and fits its unique organizational environment. For some boards, this may result only in minor adjustments to how they implement a policy-based governance-type model or enhance how the CEO communicates with the board. For others, it may require amending the bylaws. It may lead to how board meeting agendas or time frames are structured. It may result in the recruitment of new board members with needed skill sets. It may require an honest conversation as to whether the current CEO continues to have the right skill sets for a rapidly changing world. It may require creating opportunities for social interaction among board members and between board members and the senior leadership team. It may entail a new commitment to board governance as the board and CEO openly acknowledge that their current practices are less than ideal. It may include acknowledging that their brand was better suited for a past generation. It may include a difficult conversation about whether some board members are placing their personal agendas ahead of effective board governance.

CHAPTER 9

Intentionality

The art of good governance requires intentionality. A board must periodically discuss what type of board it wants to be. Is its primary role to provide oversight, what Carter and Lorsch, in *Back to the Drawing Board*, refer to as a *watchdog* board? Or does the board want to provide more of a hands-on leadership approach to guide the future direction of their organization? If so, the board would adopt a *pilot* role as described by Carter and Lorsch.[17]

The answer will depend on a host of variables, including the sophistication of the board; the complexity and geographic breadth of the organization; the industry that the organization operates within; the expectations of various stakeholders, including funders and accrediting agencies; the talent of the senior leadership team; the amount of time available for board members to devote to their board responsibilities; and the specific point of the history of the organization. No one answer fits all boards. Even healthy watchdog-styled boards will find on occasion the benefit of drilling deep into a particular issue or opportunity that has presented itself. What is motivating is that the board has the freedom to define its role today, knowing that its role may also necessarily change over time.

I served on a board that wrestled with this very question and initially decided that it wanted to fulfill its role as a pilot board. We quickly learned, however—and to the relief of the CEO—that we simply didn't possess the time or requisite skill sets to be effective in this enhanced role. The truth is that our collective egos overshadowed the reality of our situation. The industry and organization were too complex, and the external environment was changing too rapidly for part-time board members to make timely, effective strategic decisions. Strategy necessarily needed to stay within the purview of the senior leadership team, with the board playing the role of providing wise counsel as it also continued in its effective role as a watchdog board.

The role of the board may also change over time. In my experience, the answer isn't either-or but rather what makes the most sense at a specific time in an organization's history. Situations that may necessitate a change in the intensity of board oversight could, for example, include a time when the board and CEO are considering making a huge bet-the-organization decision about its future mission or an all-in bet on replacing bricks and mortar with a technology strategy. Or it could involve replacing a long-time CEO with a new leader. Or the organization may be struggling for its very survival, and all hands are needed on deck.

A board may also decide to slightly shift its governance oversight to adjust to the changing times. As an example, one board of a large nonprofit organization recently amended its personnel committee charter to provide this committee (as opposed to the CEO) with the ultimate authority to approve all compensation packages for the other members of the C-suite, including the chief operating officer, chief financial officer, and chief external relations officer. It wasn't that the board didn't trust the CEO's judgment. Rather, the organization had evolved and, to secure the right type of leadership, it often needed to recruit its top talent from the for-profit sector, which increased the complexity of compensation packages going forward. The board correctly understood that from a risk-management perspective, it was now their fiduciary responsibility to review the independently verified compensation data so that the organization could legally and ethically demonstrate to the IRS and other stakeholders that its compensation practices were justified and based on best practices. This pivot made sense as board members who served on this committee possessed a greater sophistication in creating compensation packages than their CEO. It also took the pressure off the CEO as the sole decision maker.

The art of governance requires the board, working with the CEO, to intentionally determine how to best monitor the performance of both the organization and the CEO, which categories of major decisions it wants to be involved in, what duties outside of its official governance responsibilities it will require each board member to participate in, what its role is in providing strategic advice and counsel to the CEO, and the depth of its ongoing succession planning. While each board will answer these questions somewhat differently, the best practice is for the CEO and the board to intentionally set time aside to engage in conversation regarding their respective roles as they continue in their quest to create an effective partnership of shared oversight. It will also require an honest assessment of how much time it will take for the board to properly fulfill its role once decisions are made.

More important than the ultimate answer of where the board lies on the pendulum swing of being a watchdog versus a pilot board is the willingness of the board and CEO to engage in this conversation. A question to ponder: is this one of your proverbial elephants in the room, or is there currently common agreement between the board and CEO? Knowing that there is never a perfect, final answer, the value often lies in continually engaging in a transparent, trust-filled conversation as to how the board can best add value to the organization.

If done with intentionality, the result is the creation of a continuous flywheel that keeps adding value. If both the board and the CEO commit to the art of governance, the science of their governance model will also be strengthened and the resulting payoff potentially significant. Creating a culture of intentionality that recognizes the importance of the art of good governance will strengthen the relationship between the board and CEO. It will also lead to an enhanced ability to understand, predict, and proactively respond to external changes in the environment. Both the CEO and the board will be empowered to utilize their respective strengths to effectively move the organization forward. By focusing on the art of governance, the science of how your organization should be governed will also be enhanced.

A word of caution: it takes two to tango. No amount of focus on the scientific aspect of governance will be enough if the art of governance is ignored or sabotaged. A board will have great difficulty effectively fulfilling its role if the CEO doesn't want it to be involved. At least in the short term, there are simply too many levers at a CEO's disposal to keep the board at a distance. Board members necessarily depend on the CEO to want to be their partner in this governance dance.

I served on a board where we had just selected a new CEO. The previous CEO and board often clashed. The previous CEO simply did not trust the board's ability to make good decisions and so attempted to keep us at a distance. During the interview process, the soon-to-be-selected

CEO and the board discussed what good governance meant from each perspective and committed to making the relationship work going forward. Together we decided that, for the time being, it would be a best practice to separate the CEO and chair roles. The board selected a chair who had a reputation for integrity and possessed significant emotional intelligence and maturity. With both the new CEO and board now fully committed, slowly but surely a strong sense of trust reemerged between the senior leadership team and the board, which allowed them to move forward in unison. This also allowed the board and senior staff to utilize their individual and collective strengths as they added value to the organization via the governance process.

Another board was tasked to select a new leader to replace a long-tenured CEO. It became clear to the newer board members that the previous board had been asleep at the wheel, functioning merely as a rubber stamp for the outgoing CEO. The decade-long combination of an ineffective board and a less-than-competent CEO resulted in placing this storied institution at great risk. It had failed to adjust to the changing external realities and was tottering close to bankruptcy. Fortunately, the new board and CEO committed to becoming true partners, moving forward. Because all hands were needed on deck in this situation, the board committed itself to serve as a pilot board as they and the CEO attempted to save their organization. It is a vivid reminder that both good governance and good leadership matter and are intertwined. You simply cannot have one without the other.

CHAPTER 10

The Art of Finding the Right Balance in Governing

Most boards meet no more than a total of 50–75 hours a year. Even the more complex, publicly traded, Fortune 500 boards rarely meet for more than 100–200 hours a year. Given this reality, effective boards must intentionally design a governance model that allows them to make the most of their limited time. How will the board fulfill its legal responsibilities? What mix of time should be spent thinking strategically? What data is needed to help the board do its job? What are the current obstacles that prevent the board from effectively fulfilling its role? How can a board effectively utilize technology? Does the rhythm, length, and frequency of board meetings promote board effectiveness? What is the appropriate size of the board?

The baseline for every board is that it must fulfill its mandated fiduciary responsibilities. Typically, during new board-member orientation, new board members are educated as to what it means to fulfill the board's duties of loyalty, care, and obedience.[18] Good boards and their CEO, working together, will create an appropriate roadmap for how this gets accomplished. Questions might include these:

- **What internal controls guard against the potential for theft or misuse?**

- **Does an employee have a safe mechanism to report any wrongdoing without fear of reprisal?**

- How are board meetings structured to guard against organizational drift?

- How often does the board review the financial results?

- What metrics are in place to determine organizational success?

- What are the potential enterprise risks? How is the board informed or involved?

- Does each committee have a charter that outlines its responsibilities?

- What is the role, if any, of an executive committee?

- How is the relationship between the CEO and the board defined?

- Is there enough clarity? Or should attention be given to updating the parameters of this relationship, preferably in writing?

The complexity and depth of the roadmap will depend on the needs of each organization. Much of the rhythm of governance work can be placed on a calendar and monitored by an appropriate individual, in some instances the CEO or possibly a paralegal or an executive assistant. This individual will work with the board chair, committee chairs, CEO, and appropriate staff to ensure that the various tasks, such as meeting with outside auditors, distributing written board reports, updating organizational scorecards, providing monthly or quarterly financial statements, and conducting the annual evaluation of the CEO are accomplished.

The art of fulfilling one's fiduciary responsibility also includes possessing the acumen to be an effective board member. Most board members are hesitant to request that they receive further board education. It may simply not be part of the culture, or they may be worried that either the CEO or their peers will think less of them for asking. Best practice includes intentionally bringing the board into the conversation as to what would be an effective approach for their continuing education. It may include a deep dive into a specific program or line of business, attending an industry conference, or visiting a program site. It may include further education as to what financial levers the organization has at its disposal. The CEO and the board chair may decide to bring in an industry expert to share the latest trends with the board.

As CEO and as a board member, I have found value in the joint board-CEO exercise of creating and then periodically reviewing a Board-CEO Policy Manual that clearly defines what the CEO is expected and authorized to do. The manual delineates what responsibilities are the CEO's and what responsibilities fall under the board's purview. Included in this manual are a description of the role and responsibilities of being a board member as well as a summary of the duties that the board has assigned to itself, such as, the purchase and sale of real estate or the approval of the auditors and annual audit.

I have worked with manuals as short as ten pages and as detailed as ninety pages. Some follow the Carver Model and are expressed in negative language as to what the CEO is not allowed to do. Others, such as my organization, utilize a hybrid that establishes the CEO's authority and responsibilities in positive language. No matter what the practice, this manual serves as a living document that the board and CEO regularly review, with both having the freedom to recommend changes for board approval as the needs of the organization evolve.

The goal of any written board document, whether a policy manual or a board committee charter, is to create a healthy understanding of respective roles and responsibilities, clarity on what is and isn't allowed, and an environment where the CEO feels empowered to innovate and take appropriate risks in pursuit of the agreed-upon mission. This mutual understanding of clarity of responsibility will, in turn, enhance the efficiency and effectiveness of the governance model as well as garner trust among its leaders.

On occasion, a board will be asked to decide on a major bet-the-farm strategic initiative or select a new CEO. I was a relatively new board member of a Fortune 500 company when the board voted to merge with another Fortune 500 organization. This was our bet-the-farm decision that necessarily required additional time and attention from the board. However, what struck me after the merger was that it was at least two years before the board became deeply involved in making another major decision. The board appropriately understood that we were in a season where management was tasked with merging operations and systems and the board wisely allowed management to take the lead in creating a unified company. The board focused its attention on the nuts and bolts of governing as it created a new governance model for the combined organization.

Depending on the season of an organization's life, board decisions will vary in terms of magnitude. Creating a strategic vision, making a major capital commitment, acquiring another organization, establishing an endowment-investment policy, approving a budget, and planning for effective succession are all part and parcel of the shared responsibilities between the board and CEO. The art of a board member is knowing when to wear the hat of a listener, adviser, cheerleader, active participant, or decision maker.

CHAPTER 11

The Art of Creating an Effective, Diverse Board

The art of creating an effective, diverse board is dependent on knowing that your quest will never be finished. The board and the CEO must intentionally identify which skill sets and cultural influences are most important at this specific time in the organization's history, where the gaps are, and what the most effective way to identify, recruit, and onboard each board member is.

BoardSource, the influential nonprofit governance institute, surveyed more than 800 nonprofit CEOs and board chairs. It found that 49 percent of CEOs said that they don't have the right boards to establish trust in the communities they serve, most board members were ill-informed about the ecosystems in which the nonprofit organization operated, most boards were not ethnically or gender diverse, and many boards did not recognize that providing strategic direction should be their top priority.[19]

Creating an effective and appropriately diverse board takes work. It will take more effort to find the right candidate, as the person you seek doesn't necessarily run in your circles. Depending on the nuances of the organization, diversity in its broadest forms—ethnicity, age, gender, religion, life experience, profession, personality, specific industry experience, geography—has the potential to add value to a board. With most boards ranging in size from eight to twelve members, it is of course virtually impossible to create a perfectly diverse board. The art of governance necessitates that one prioritizes what is most important at the time, knowing that the board's landscape will continue to evolve and require new backgrounds and skill sets.

It is increasingly a given that board diversity matters. An often-cited study by McKinsey and Company, a management consulting firm, found that companies with diverse boards outperformed those with more homogeneous boards.[20] The investment firm Goldman Sachs announced that it would no longer invest in any initial public offering that has an all-white, male board.[21] Other foundations have announced that they will no longer provide funding to nonprofit organizations that do not have a sufficiently diverse board or executive team.

Designing an effective, diverse board is almost always a shared responsibility in which both the board and the CEO need to be proactively involved. A confident CEO will recommend prospective board members who have a wide variety of perspectives and experiences. She knows that this will only improve the organization and her skill sets. She will most likely want at least one board member with CEO experience because, unless one has served in that role, it is difficult to comprehend the enormity and complexity of the position.

The CEO is also typically best positioned to come across prospective candidates, as he has the most interaction with engaged stakeholders. Good governance dictates that it is appropriate for the CEO to take the lead as long as that lead is counterbalanced by an engaged board and/or a strong board or committee chair. An emotionally intelligent board leader will intuitively know if the CEO is focused on seeking the best board members to improve the organization or is seeking to populate the board with yes-men or -women.

The ideal process, of course, is a combination of both science and art. The science comes into play as a board identifies which skill sets are most needed to enhance the collective wisdom of the board; for example, legal, human resources, strategic, fundraising, or technology expertise. The art comes into play as they seek to evaluate the emotional intelligence of the board member and the passion she has for the mission of the organization, and also as they strive for appropriate diversity.

The danger in any process, no matter how well designed, is that there is a tendency for CEOs and board members to identify and recommend board candidates with whom they enjoy some sort of familiarity or comfort level. The prospective board member may come from the same neighborhood, have the same political perspective, or be of the same age group or income level. The danger is that groupthink then becomes the norm as board members with homogeneous backgrounds populate the board, even if on the outside they might appear to be appropriately diverse.

The primary disadvantage of a homogeneous board, whether it be all of the same sex, generation, ethnic background, professional experiences, church affiliation, neighborhood, or wealth strata, is that, by definition, it narrows the board's worldview in a way that potentially can be harmful to the organization. And even if a board is heterogeneous in terms of gender, diversity, and experience, it may continue to be homogeneous in terms of its worldview.

It is in the organization's interest to have board members who hold competing worldviews because it allows for a broader conversation to occur about the various risks associated with a specific strategy. One organization that relies heavily on federal funding found it advantageous to have board members with both Democrat and Republican political leanings sitting at the table. This is also why many social service organizations proactively recruit board members who, in the past, were clients; for example, those who grew up in the foster-care system. They simply have a perspective that those of us who were blessed to grow up within a stable family structure will never have. Similarly, it is increasingly recognized that, with technology being so vital to virtually every organization's success, there is value to having board members who represent different generations and technological sophistication present at the table.

For me, diversity includes so much more than ensuring that a board has a diverse array of gender and ethnic representation, as important as that is. Rather, diversity is about the uniqueness that each of us represents and how we bring our individual experiences to the table to create value and drive outcomes. Boards and leadership teams that have a diverse array of life experiences, professional backgrounds, and worldviews are less likely to succumb to groupthink and are more likely to create a sharper vision of the organization's future.

Creating a diverse board often brings about the need for increased sensitivity. Sometimes a person from a different background doesn't appear to quite fit in or isn't familiar with the cultural milieu of the organization he or she has been asked to join. Existing board members often aren't even aware there is a "secret handshake" that signals you are a part of the tribe. That "secret handshake" may be the unspoken dress code, traditional golf outing, off-color jokes, common table prayer, or annual cigar ritual that unintentionally marginalizes the outsider. The art of creating a diverse board is to be cognizant of what makes everyone feel comfortable and then create an environment that does so. This could include assigning a mentor, abandoning previous traditions, creating new inclusive rituals, and intentionally creating space to hear their stories. Most important is to not immediately dismiss others' comments because they don't fit within your worldview.

The fact that a person is different is exactly why you invited that person to join the board. The art of creating a diverse board that works effectively together is to create time for board members to get to know one another, to ensure that all become aligned on what strategic priorities define success, and to have an emotionally intelligent board chair who is adept at creating a culture that supports healthy and honest debate, which will ultimately create an environment where governance is indeed a competitive advantage.

I would add the category of *gadfly* to the definition of having an artfully designed diverse board. When trust exists among the board and between the board and CEO, a dissenter—someone who possesses emotional intelligence and is willing to appropriately rock the boat, take the other side, bring up the elephant in the room, question the soundness of a certain strategy—may on occasion become a thorn in the side of a CEO or board chair but has the potential to add great value to a boardroom and an organization's strategy.

The act of questioning the majority or commonly accepted view can ultimately lead to subsequent dialogue at both the staff and board level that is original, creative, and eye-opening, often leading to enhanced strategies and outcomes. I chaired the board of an organization that had an outspoken, emotionally intelligent gadfly as a board member. He was constantly challenging the sacred cows. After one meeting, he commented to me, "You know, Kurt, we didn't move the box forward today. We merely rearranged the pieces inside the box." He took his role seriously and had a deep passion for the organization. He wasn't going to waste his time being a rubber stamp. Rather, he was going to offer his reflections, knowing that he was only one member of a board but also believing that this is what he was called to do and that it would be a dereliction of duty for him not to.

While the CEO and I spent a considerable amount of time managing this board member—including one instance when I received several voicemails from him between the time my post-board meeting flight took off and subsequently landed—in retrospect, the CEO, myself, and the entire board would all acknowledge that this individual added value to the organization. As a result of his wise counsel, the CEO became a better leader and the skill sets of this board chair were enhanced.

CHAPTER 12

The Art of Creating an Effective Board— Questions to Ponder

While the author assumes that each board is cognizant of, at least in theory, the ideal makeup of its board, a few additional questions may spur further discussion. For example:

- Should organizations that serve primarily lower-income communities have representation from the communities they serve?

- How important is it for an organization that provides education, health care, or foster-care services to have board members who understand the industry?

- How important is it for a board to have at least one member who is a client who has benefited from the services provided?

- Are there one or two board members sophisticated enough to thoroughly understand the organization's financials and the various levers that management has at its disposal to drive the revenue and expense sides of the business?

- Are female board members merely included to fill a quota? Or is there an intentional strategy in terms of quantity and quality to allow for their fresh and wise counsel?

- Is there at least one board member with C-suite experience, someone who has been through this before, who can serve as a mentor and offer wisdom to the CEO?

During the past five years, we have witnessed a sea change in how technology is impacting every organization. Virtually every boardroom will have discussions that center around the use of technology such as social media, data analytics, and artificial intelligence to enhance the customer experience or transform business models. Board discussions on these topics won't be of use to the leadership team unless there are board members who possess sophisticated acumen in this area. Also, not having technology experts as a board skill set opens the organization up to another set of risks, as it will be unable to fulfill its responsibility of risk-management oversight as it relates to cybersecurity, technological disruptions, and investments in technology. Given this new reality, would it be wise for the CEO to reach out to younger employees to seek suggestions for potential board members?

A board I am involved with recently appointed a young executive of a growth-stage technology company to replace a board member with more of a typical Fortune 500 résumé as the organization continues to execute its strategy to deliver a larger percentage of services via technology to its clients. A historically ideal board candidate may no longer be appropriate. It may be in the organization's best interest to take a chance on candidates who may be a little bit younger, more entrepreneurial, and tech-savvy, albeit with less board experience. What implications does this have on an organization's new board-member orientation and continuing education process?

Board members are also increasingly called to serve as advisers to the CEO when it comes to strategy or an emerging issue that seemingly appears out of nowhere. Many well-qualified board members simply do not have the strategic chops to be of value to a CEO in this fashion. Having several trusted mentors on the board that a CEO can call on to discuss strategic alternatives is becoming more invaluable. Which members of your board fill this role for the CEO? As successful CEOs recognize their boards as a competitive asset as opposed to a necessary evil, the art of recruiting board members who have the potential to provide sound strategic counsel will be an increasingly competitive advantage.

As boards continue to become more diverse, often, given the diversity of backgrounds, individual board-member feedback to the CEO and senior leadership team may differ in perspective and recommendations. The value of this seemingly conflicting advice is that it provides the organizational leaders with diverse viewpoints, which, in turn, allows them to make more informed decisions with the information available. Often it is more valuable for a board to provide perspective rather than direction, knowing that the CEO will benefit from this wide-ranging conversation. It is also why possessing soft skills such as empathy, communication, adaptability, and emotional intelligence are increasingly nonnegotiable components of being an effective board member and CEO.

The individual and collective talents, passions, experiences, emotional intelligence, wisdom, and skill sets of the board matter if a board is to add value to the CEO and organization. I had the privilege of serving as a consultant for an excellent CEO who had inherited a well-meaning board entrusted to oversee a large continuum-of-care nonprofit retirement community. Under its bylaws, the organization was governed by board members appointed by a consortium of churches. The various congregations would typically add this task to their voter's meeting agenda and inquire if anyone was interested in serving as a board member for the coming year. Several were selected by their congregation because they actively volunteered their time at the retirement community. While a couple of board members had been small business owners before their retirement, most possessed little relevant business experience.

It quickly became clear that these sincere board members simply did not have the expertise to assess various strategic options, including whether it was in the organization's best interest to merge with another faith-based organization. After going through a daylong strategic retreat, they acknowledged their collective deficiencies and put together a plan to appoint a more sophisticated board. Because they collectively possessed a passion for the organization and exhibited humility and emotional intelligence, they acknowledged the gaps I gently raised with them during our time together. To their credit, they were committed to doing what was right. In the words of one, "We just didn't know any better. No one told us."

CHAPTER 13

Values, Passion, and Emotional Intelligence

The art of creating an effective board goes deeper than checking off the appropriate boxes. The art also focuses on whether the board has the right collective fit. When we sit around the family Christmas dinner, we don't necessarily have to always agree on topics that get raised, such as politics or religion. However, for a healthy family dynamic, all members must possess a mutuality of trust, similar underlying values, and an unbridled passion for and commitment to the success of the collective family. The same is true for a board. An organization can't just look for, say, an attorney of a certain ethnic origin and check that box. The choice must be part of a comprehensive strategy that includes whether this individual will be an appropriate fit and has a passion for the mission of the organization.

There are three nonnegotiables for every prospective board member:

1. **Is a person of good character**

2. **Possesses a passion for the mission of the organization**

3. **Is willing to place his ego aside in service to the organization**

The art of governance understands that an individual's résumé may enable the person to be considered for a leadership or board role. However, this will merely serve as a baseline for further consideration. What will set the CEO and the board apart from their peers in relation to effective board governance is, in large part, how effectively they can manage themselves and their relationships. In this capacity, emotional intelligence is a nonnegotiable skill set as individuals with significant emotional intelligence competencies will possess high self-management and emotional self-awareness skills that allow them to focus on achieving long-term goals. Possessing an abundance of emotional intelligence also positively impacts an individual's ability to relate to others. Emotional intelligence includes skills such as empathy, organizational awareness, and an ability to influence. As a board is unique in that it is required to function as a group, the art of creating an effective board demands that we populate the seats around the table with individuals who collectively possess an abundance of emotional intelligence.

Organizations also possess their own unique culture of emotional intelligence. Engaged boards will assess how effectively their organization relates to other stakeholders.

+ **Are they considered a good partner that can be trusted?**

+ **Who holds the informal power within the organization?**

+ **Does a climate of fear exist within the organization?**

+ **Are the employees passionate about their work?**

+ **Is senior leadership working well together as a team?**

Being organizationally aware from this perspective allows board members to have better insight as to how they can best support, what changes may ultimately need to be made, who are the influencers, and, most important, what is the art of the possible.

There are times when an organization, to its detriment, seemingly wears blinders when seeking a specific type of board member. For example, nonprofit organizations often fail to add value when attempting to recruit to their boards wealthy or high-profile members of the community who have no ties to the organization. Stanford University surveyed boards of directors of nonprofit organizations; the findings showed that almost half of the boards required board members to fundraise. Of these boards, 90 percent of the respondents considered fundraising as important or more important than their governance obligations as board members.[22] What is often forgotten is that the primary purpose of the board is not to maximize the organization's fundraising tally. Rather, its main role is to effectively govern the organization. Should a board member make a financial contribution based on her financial situation? Absolutely. Should a board member be asked to introduce the organization to others within her circle of influence? Yes. Should it be a primary consideration of who should be recruited on the board? My experience says no if it negatively impacts the board's ability to fulfill its primary governance role.

Asking a wealthy individual to serve on the board is often the least effective way to recruit a potential donor. The question to ask is, Would the wealthy or well-connected individual be a good board member even if he wasn't wealthy or well-connected? Does the person have the requisite skill sets, emotional intelligence, and passion to enhance the governance of the organization? Good governance and its relationship to the success of an organization is much too important for an organization to waste a board seat solely because of the size of a board member's bank account. It is demeaning to that individual, who is cognizant of why you are seeking her out. It speaks volumes about the organization's perspective of the value of good board governance. A better alternative may be to utilize this individual's skills by creating other less formal structures for her to become involved, such as on an advisory board, a volunteer opportunity, or a fundraising committee that supports the organization.

CHAPTER 14

Being a Good Board Member Takes Commitment

Admittedly, there were times when I, as CEO, would meet with a potential board member and highlight that this request to serve on the board would not take too much of his time. I emphasized the four meetings a year, a few conference calls, and the email updates aspect of board responsibility. I was more interested in getting a yes and figuring it out later. And, if I am completely honest, at times during my career as a CEO, I worked behind the scenes to ensure that we didn't select board members who had too much time on their hands, as I was convinced that they would only get in the way.

To be part of a team that becomes a competitive advantage, today's board members must be willing to devote a substantial amount of time to this typically voluntary role. Truly understanding the business, grappling with the ever-changing external environment, and building a relationship of trust with the CEO and other board members takes commitment. It may mean attending conferences, reading trade journals, and visiting programs or facilities as part of the education process. Whether for-profit or nonprofit, gone are the days when an individual could effectively simultaneously serve on numerous boards. It is the responsibility of the CEO and the board leadership to intentionally engage in an honest dialogue with a prospective board member as to the breadth and depth necessary to serve effectively.

Historically, most CEOs defined board meeting success as ensuring that the agenda was appropriate for the issues at hand, the governance-related duties were accomplished, and the meeting was productive. The goal was to maintain an agreement to continue with their strategic vision and not allow the directors to get too far into the weeds. Increasingly, the most effective CEOs have embraced a new mindset. Just as important as creating a governance model that allows board members to fulfill their fiduciary obligations, best-of-class CEOs are asking their boards to focus on the pressing organizational challenges of the moment, knowing that they will benefit from the boards' input. For this strategy to be of value, CEOs are increasingly evaluating whether their board composition is appropriate for their organization in the future, making the necessary adjustments while simultaneously continuing to bring existing directors to the next level.

One nonnegotiable skill set for virtually all board members is the ability to understand what drives the organization's programmatic and/ or financial outcomes. What various levers does the organization have at its disposal to achieve its desired missional path? What are the organization's major strategies? How might changes in the external environment impact those strategies? Some board members will, of course, have more programmatic acumen and less financial background, or vice versa. What all need to possess, however, is the capacity and willingness to lean into their board role so they can add value to the organization.

A question that I am often asked is, Given the increased time commitment and complexity of its work, should a nonprofit organization provide some sort of monetary stipend to the members of its board? The answer that I provide in most situations is no. The good news is that board members are choosing to serve to make a difference in their community. The idea of financial gain is simply not part of the equation. Charitable nonprofit organizations are tasked to serve the public good and should not enrich any person or group of individuals. While compensating a nonprofit board member is not forbidden under federal law, it is in some state jurisdictions. Also, in certain situations, compensated board members might lose immunity from lawsuits filed against the organization.[23]

Despite these caveats, there may be reasons for certain organizations to explore this idea further. On occasion, a large health-care system, art museum, or foundation may decide that it is a good governance practice to compensate its board members due to the complexity of the needed oversight and the special expertise required. One foundation that I am aware of does not monetarily compensate its directors but rather provides each with a yearly stipend to donate to the charity or charities of each person's choice. In another innovative experiment, A Blade of Grass, a New York nonprofit for socially engaged art, was forced to lay off almost all its employees during the pandemic and instead reconstituted its board to be comprised of six artists and art workers, with each of them receiving an honorarium for his or her work. The rationale for this innovative change was that the new board is more committed, is able to be more creative and nimble, and truly understands what is at stake.[24] Time will tell if this is a successful pivot. It is an excellent example of an organization creatively embracing the art of governance.

CHAPTER 15

Size Matters

The size of the board matters. Some nonprofit organizations such as universities and museums have boards as large as forty members. While this may make sense as part of a historic fundraising strategy, the reality is that even in these situations, the actual governance of such an institution typically falls upon a much smaller group of six to twelve members. Maybe the biggest disadvantage to a large board is the tendency for some members to disengage. Psychologists refer to this as *social loafing*. This occurs when a board member relies on others to take the lead. A board member who serves on a board with fewer board members is more likely to become more engaged because she understands that her participation matters.

An important governance trend is taking place. Boards are increasingly becoming smaller in size. For some organizations, there is a growing recognition that from the perspective of good governance, less sometimes is better.[25] Sought-after board members have limited time, and those who are successfully recruited want to make a difference, which is easier to accomplish with a smaller board. It has also become increasingly difficult to recruit outstanding board members. Board members have become more selective before agreeing to board service. Understanding that this responsibility will take time and comes with some risk, they do their due diligence. This dating dance has become more complicated on both sides. Increased attention is being paid to crafting an appropriate combination of skill sets, personalities, and diversity to be seated around the table. By intentionally seeking the right talent, there is less of a need for quantity.

There are additional benefits to having a smaller board. It is easier to focus on recruiting quality board candidates when the board and CEO know that they need to recruit only one or two candidates a year. A smaller board also makes it more manageable for the CEO to build a culture of trust and understanding with each board member. The flip side is that each board member must be all in and, depending on the complexity and governance structure of the organization, may have to serve on more than one committee. It will mean that each board member will need to be engaged and held accountable.

As organizations evolve, the size of the board should periodically be reassessed. I have served on boards as small as four and as large as eighteen. A good rule of thumb is that there is value to having the board be as small as is feasible, with six to twelve typically the sweet spot. The smaller the board, the easier it is to engage in robust conversations and ultimately reach a consensus. As my organization transitioned from a board that represented various interested stakeholders to a completely independent board, the board made the appropriate decision to reduce its size from eighteen to twelve. I currently serve on the board of a start-up nonprofit organization, which when formed, began with four board members. We recently decided to increase the size of our board to six by bringing on a CEO with significant community contacts as well as a younger board member with significant start-up and technology experience. Both quickly added value as they view the world from a unique perspective.

CHAPTER 16

The Art of Creating an Effective Board-CEO Relationship

There is a structural yet necessary tension between the CEO's role to lead the organization and the board's role to oversee the performance of the CEO. This can lead to unintended consequences if not acknowledged and openly discussed. In a healthy environment, there will be times when the relationship will feel like an equal partnership, situations when the CEO is empowered to make the ultimate decision, and circumstances when the board will need to take charge as it fulfills its role and/or holds the CEO accountable. It is a delicate dance in which partners take turns taking the lead. To continue the metaphor, toes are less likely to get stepped on if it is clear who is empowered to lead in each situation.

As a starting point, both must come to the table understanding that their respective roles are of service and shared partnership. If a board member perceives his only role in a boardroom is to serve as a judge and does not embrace his other roles as an adviser and partner in mission, a fearful CEO may be less than forthcoming. The mission of the organization must always remain front and center. It is the collective responsibility of the board and the CEO to further this mission as they intentionally hold each other and themselves accountable.

As an example, I served on a board where the organization unexpectedly missed its financial goals by a wide margin and finished the year with a sizeable loss. To the leadership's credit, they approached the issue head-on, kept the board informed, and made numerous necessary changes. When it came time to present the next year's budget to the board, the CFO recommended no annual salary increases for any of the employees. The staff made this recommendation in part as one piece of the puzzle needed to make up part of the previous year's losses. The board also sensed that the staff was recommending this course of action because they believed this is what the board expected, not what was the best decision going forward.

The board asked several probing questions, including what the average pay increase was for other nonprofit organizations in the area. The answer was 3 percent. Another board member inquired whether the staff had factored into the budget the cost of potential increased turnover as well as a deterioration in employee morale, which would lead to a decrease in employee engagement. At the end of a thoughtful discussion, both the board and staff leadership agreed that a better solution was to provide the employees who were not classified as managers or executives a 2 percent increase across the board. While maybe not a perfect solution, the result of this healthy dialogue was deemed better by all. It is an example of the board and staff engaging in a trust-infused dialogue about what is best for the long-term health of the organization while still sending an appropriate message that no organization can tolerate ongoing financial losses.

From a legal perspective, the board is in charge. The CEO reports to the board. However, unless a board decides to exercise its nuclear option of firing the CEO, the reality is that it is typically the CEO who possesses most of the power. This fact was brought home to me every time a board member jokingly called me *boss* even though he was technically my boss. When I reminded them of this fact, some laughed as if it were a joke. It is an implicit acknowledgment that day to day, with a few agreed-upon exceptions, the CEO is in charge and that in many situations a board will be effective only if the CEO wants it to be.

Once a board grasps this truly complex relationship with its CEO, it will be able to chart a course that allows it to effectively govern. One rule of thumb is that a board and CEO will typically operate at least 90 percent of the time as partners, with the CEO knowing that there will be a small portion of authority legally reserved to the board to necessarily act as *boss*. These situations include evaluating the CEO, determining executive compensation, overseeing the audit process, purchasing or selling real estate, approving the organization's mission, making key pivots in organizational strategy, selecting the next CEO, and managing times of crisis.

For this relationship to work, it is incumbent that the CEO invest a significant portion of her time in building a trust-filled relationship with each board member. New CEOs are often initially not fully cognizant of the unique characteristics that make up the board-CEO relationship. This dynamic is different than their relationship with their direct reports. When a CEO engages with a board, she is, for the most part, engaging with a group of peers. For a CEO to be successful, she needs to treat her board as peers as she both learns from, educates, listens to, and persuades her board members to collectively craft an agreed-upon vision. In my later years as a CEO, I looked forward to my regular board-member calls, which I viewed as part of my sensing mechanism, and often found that our conversations led to better organizational outcomes.

A constructive relationship is more likely to occur if the CEO devotes sufficient energy to developing a trust-filled relationship with each board member. While this takes intentionality, it is worth the commitment and often leads to a healthy CEO-board relationship, which can be a stepping stone to extraordinary organizational outcomes. This garnered relationship equity will also be available to the CEO when the board is deliberating over a difficult issue and the CEO can utilize her emotional-intelligence skills to persuade skeptical board members that her proposed plan of action is in the best interests of the organization.

Proactively building these relationships can often save a CEO during times of difficulty. An organization recently merged with a similar-sized organization. After the merger, the CEO soon discovered that for every new sale they made, the newly merged organization incurred a loss. Worse, the more the organization sold, the larger the losses. Because of how the organization's commission-based compensation system was designed, volume wasn't its friend. Fortunately, to prepare for the merger, the CEO had worked hard to develop a relationship with each board member and had built up a reservoir of trust. He and his team were able to come to the newly formed board, explain the problem, and offer proposed solutions. Although the new board admittedly was surprised by the news, collectively, with minimal blame, decisions were made that ensured the long-term financial health of the organization.

For governance to truly be a competitive advantage, a board member's willingness to be an authentic servant leader—no matter what the personal cost—must be front and center. On occasion, a situation develops where a CEO—sometimes due to his force of personality or his track record of achieving results—becomes larger than life. As a result, his board abdicates its responsibility and becomes too subservient or subconsciously ignores the flashing warning signs. Or maybe an individual board member possesses virtually all the informal authority because she is the founder of the organization, a significant donor, or an influential stakeholder. Or, in certain organizations (museums, symphonies, and universities, for example), it is a professional honor to be selected to their boards. Board members may be unwilling to rock the boat because they don't want to lose their influential position. Organizations in which boards intentionally or unintentionally abdicate their fiduciary duties typically experience a breakdown in the governance process. If left unchecked, such abdication can ultimately impede the effectiveness of or even destroy an organization.

Boards and CEOs that have the most productive working relationships are also those who have taken the time to get to know each other. To foster these relationships, an easy first step is for the board chair and CEO to arrange for board members and key members of the senior leadership team to eat dinner together, perhaps the evening before a board meeting. Once I joined a board where, from the start, I noticed that the various factions of the board would eat by themselves the night before a meeting, cementing their strategy. This led to an atmosphere of mistrust in the boardroom, where each board member had allies he knew well but a host of others that he simply didn't know on a personal level, yet knew they were part of the *other* clique. A new board chair changed this culture. By having dinner together, I found that a board member I did not know well shared a common passion for wine. With others, including members of the senior leadership team, I learned about their families, experiences, and interests. It allowed me to better place myself in their shoes. What resulted is that as we got to know one another personally, we gained an enhanced mutual trust and respect for one another's integrity and skill sets. This translated into a renewed sense of partnership as collectively we worked to enhance the mission of the organization.

CHAPTER 17

The Art of Being an Effective Board Member

The four nonnegotiable components of being an effective board member are to possess a passion for the mission, be willing to commit the time, place the needs of the organization first, and have the expertise or background to effectively contribute.

Being an effective board member also requires having the ability to possess emotional awareness as it relates to one's board role. It means understanding the difference between informed oversight and overreach. It understands that one of the goals of an open board dialogue is to welcome differing viewpoints to discover a shared solution that the entire board will support after a decision is made. An emotionally aware board chair understands that the *power* that comes with her board position rests in the collective board; that her focus should be to use her position to ensure all voices are heard and that collaborative solutions are reached. An effective board member also understands that his sole purpose is to serve the community, collaboratively agree upon a clear mission and vision, and effectively oversee a measurable strategic plan that fulfills its mission.

The art of being an effective board member includes knowing that you will never be a perfect board member. In reading one of a myriad of board governance books, I counted ninety-three different tasks that the author believed a board should be responsible for. I consider myself an effective board member and acknowledge it would be impossible for me to fulfill every listed obligation. While aspects of this list may be appropriate for each board, the reality is that no board or individual board member has the expertise or time available to oversee such a vast array of responsibilities. The art of governance acknowledges this quandary and solves it by creating a board-committee structure that fits its unique situation, focuses ahead on the vital current issues facing the organization, and creates clarity and appropriate policies as to what falls within the responsibility of the CEO.

Board members, not unlike outstanding CEOs, must possess a growth mindset. Carol Dweck, in *Mindset: The New Psychology of Success*,[26] explains how people who fall into this category believe that intelligence, like muscle, can be developed. Boards who individually and collectively possess this attribute will naturally want to participate in governance educational opportunities. They will want to keep abreast of the latest trends impacting the organization. Best-in-class boards will also take their self-evaluation process seriously. And, increasingly as a best practice, many boards will reach out to their senior leadership team and ask them these three questions, which will then be compiled to preserve anonymity and shared with the board chair or appropriate committee:

1. **What does the board do that you would like to see them CONTINUE?**

2. **What does the board not do that you would like to see them START?**

3. **What does the board do that you would like to see them STOP?**

A board that allows itself to become vulnerable to the senior leadership team in this way has the potential to improve the governance process of the organization and solidify the shared partnership between staff and the board.

Under most governance models, the CEO is responsible for everything other than the responsibilities that the board has reserved for itself or cannot legally delegate. The art of being a key participant of an effective board is to create systems and a board culture to ensure that the CEO and her team are both empowered and held accountable. To fulfill this role, each board member must view himself as a trustee-owner of the organization. What this means in plain English is that the organization always comes first—not your friendship with the CEO, a business relationship that might come about as the result of your board service, the fear of criticism that comes with making unpopular decisions, or the prestige you receive by serving on the board. When every conversation begins with the understanding that the organization comes first, it is easier to strategize about the elephant in the room, speak the truth in love, and hold one another and the CEO accountable. The primary role of a board member is service—often unacknowledged and sometimes unappreciated—so that collectively, a greater good is achieved.

Without a clear framework to guide the board, the board is left to its own devices. A board in such a situation is too often swayed by the larger-than-life personality of the CEO, a dominant voice or voices of the board, or the history and culture of the organization. In these situations, a board tends to become reactive, not proactive. What a board focuses on gets dictated by the various crises that appear from time to time, such as financial difficulties, census concerns, and fundraising challenges. Board members get frustrated, as it feels like they are continually playing the board-member equivalent of the popular arcade game *Whac-A-Mole*, where players whack plastic moles with a mallet as the creatures pop their heads out of burrows, but as soon as a player successfully whacks one mole, a new one pops up.

The art of governance understands this reality and focuses on creating systems that provide clarity of accountability while continually adjusting as the situation dictates and the organization evolves. As an example, one organization traditionally owned the real estate of its facility-based programs. Its board policy manual appropriately required board approval for any purchase or sale of real estate. Historically, board approval was not needed in signing office leases. Typically, their leases ranged in the low five-figure range, which, even if they closed the program and were still liable for the rent, would not place the organization at risk. However, the organization later found it advantageous to lease as opposed to buying large residential facilities and schools. This allowed it to be nimble and use less capital to create new programs. The board, after consultation with the CEO, appropriately amended the board policy manual that would require their approval if the total amount of any lease agreement exceeded $1 million. From their perspective, this was the level that could potentially place the organization at some risk if something went wrong. When both the board and the CEO are intentionally proactive in assessing what is appropriate board oversight, the role of the board becomes manageable and the organization benefits.

CHAPTER 18

The Art of Being an Effective Board Chair

One of the most important roles of the board is to select the right board chair. Too often, the chair is selected based on having seniority, volunteering for the job, donating the most money, or being good friends with the CEO. This role is simply too important for there not to be intentionality in the decision-making process. In well-governed organizations, recommending who should be elected as board chair for the coming year is within the domain of board governance or the executive committee. This allows several board members, along with the CEO, to confidentially engage in a conversation regarding the experience, time availability, and emotional intelligence of potential chair candidates and then recommend one specific candidate to the board for approval. Or a committee chair or consultant will reach out individually to each board member to receive confidential input. These types of processes prevent embarrassment and hurt feelings that can come with publicly conducting a vote among board members.

Every organization will have unique needs in what type of professional background will best serve the organization as board chair. Often, what works best for an organization is a chair that possesses a deep reservoir of emotional intelligence, previous board experience, and business acumen, typically at the C-suite level. Emotional intelligence is critical in this role, as an effective board chair must be adept at managing her feelings while adroitly reading and managing the boardroom. A successful board chair must possess the ability to bring a group of diverse individuals together to work effectively with one another. This social poise allows her to effortlessly reach out to new board members to make them feel at ease and a part of the board structure.

Daniel Goleman, in *Emotional Intelligence: Why It Can Matter More Than IQ*, describes how when people come together to collaborate—as in a board of directors—it is appropriate to think about this group in terms of having a group IQ, which is defined as "the sum total of the talents and skills of all those involved." [27] What separates the effectiveness of one group over another group with similar talents and skill sets is social harmony. The most important factor in maximizing the effectiveness of a group is its ability to create a state of internal harmony. And while a board can't be any smarter than its sum of skill sets, it has the potential to be dumber if its culture doesn't allow board members to share their talents. Goleman goes on to describe two common factors that reduce the potential and effectiveness of a high group IQ: (1) Individuals who participate too much are a drag on the overall group. They lack the social intelligence to determine what is and isn't appropriate and become too domineering. (2) Individuals who do not actively participate. They become dead weight. [28]

It is the board chair's responsibility to guard against both extremes. Strategies may include intentionally calling on those who haven't said much during a board discussion. It may also require a board chair to appropriately remind a board member that all members need an equal opportunity to participate. A boardroom culture has no room for either bullies or wallflowers. The successful board chair will also be skillful at organizing groups, mediating, and negotiating a solution that is acceptable to a group consensus; be adept at connecting to staff and board members; be a great team player; and have an intuitive ability to detect and understand others' motives, needs, feelings, and concerns.

It will be the board chair who will most likely have the most contact with the CEO between meetings. This is also the individual that the CEO will go to first when an issue arises or advice is needed. The board chair and CEO will also spend time crafting the board agenda, preparing for the meeting, and anticipating what the major topics of discussion will be. As a result, it is often the board chair who will have developed the closest relationship with the CEO and will be best positioned to pick up on potential warning signs.

- **Does he seem stressed?**

- **Has he become disengaged?**

- **Could she benefit from wise counsel on a specific issue?**

- **How is his health?**

A perceptive board chair can often proactively work to solve an issue before it becomes a crisis.

CHAPTER 19

The Art of an Effective CEO-Board Chair Relationship

In describing the relationship between the board chair and the CEO, some use the analogy of the relationship between a coach and a quarterback. Both share the same goal of winning and coming to an agreement on a game plan. It is the quarterback who plays the game and makes a myriad of heat-of-the-moment decisions. The coach, in addition to developing the quarterback, provides game-day counsel and encouragement and reserves the right to change quarterbacks if results aren't forthcoming.

From my perspective, this analogy isn't quite accurate. For me, the ideal board chair must be part friend, colleague, adviser, confidant, taskmaster, therapist, mediator, cheerleader, coach, and boss all rolled into one. Maybe the analogy of a good marriage is more appropriate. For this relationship to work, it must depend on mutual respect, trust, and support. Both must intentionally find time to communicate with each other. While personalities, experiences, and styles may be different, what spouses have in common in a healthy marriage is a shared purpose. When trust is present, conversations will naturally occur in the context of what is good for the organization.

Most CEOs live with the constant hum of anxiety that is unique to this role. The buck often truly does stop with the CEO. The relentless pressure to make payroll, raise quarterly numbers, deal with problem employees, and manage conflicting priorities of a diverse set of stakeholders makes this a 24/7/365 vocation that never gets a rest, even during the most idyllic vacation. This also speaks to the importance of the board chair possessing a reservoir of emotional intelligence since one of her roles is to support and counsel the CEO.

A good board chair will be able to communicate with empathy any concerns, gaps between expectations and performance, and advice on how to improve going forward. It requires a sensitivity to how the CEO is receiving the message and an understanding of his natural tendency to initially react defensively to criticism, no matter how well-meaning. When delivered thoughtfully, it becomes possible for a CEO, who is not typically used to receiving critical feedback, to view this as an opportunity to enhance his skill set as he moves the organization forward.

One board chair understood he had a duty to both the organization and the CEO to artfully engage in a confidential conversation regarding his heartfelt concern after he noticed that the CEO had recently gained a significant amount of weight. Something was clearly out of balance. While at first defensive, the CEO was grateful for the conversation. It allowed for honest dialogue and for the board chair to suggest some habits for the CEO to consider adopting to improve his health and mental framework. The CEO quickly got the message that the board chair both cared about him as a person and was fulfilling his role as a fiduciary to the organization.

In return, a CEO should never surprise his board chair. For a board chair to serve as an effective partner, she must be educated ahead of time on the good, the bad, and the ugly that will be discussed at the board meeting. Will the board be asked to approve any additional capital spending? Did the organization miss its financial goals? What new initiatives will be presented? Is there anything in the CEO's personal life, say an upcoming surgery, that, from a risk-management perspective, the board chair needs to know about? My board chair and I would schedule time ahead of every meeting to have dinner together or, at a minimum, talk by phone. Because we developed a trust-filled relationship, I viewed him less as a boss and more as a coach and mentor. He grew to understand my strengths and weaknesses and provide sound counsel on how to best message any new updates to the board that were consistent with our agreed-upon strategy.

CHAPTER 20

The Ground Rules

The art of governance acknowledges that a complex web of relationships exists and must intentionally be managed. This web is between board members; between the chair and the CEO; between board members and the senior leadership team; and between board members and key stakeholders. For these relationships to effectively move the organization forward, several ground rules must be established and enforced.

CEOs and their team have a natural tendency to become defensive when difficult questions are asked or their judgment is called into question. This is human nature. For board governance to become a competitive advantage, a CEO and her leadership team must learn to embrace the give-and-take of such spirited conversations, knowing that the intent is to harness the room's collective intelligence to ultimately achieve a better outcome. Directors should also feel comfortable disagreeing with one another, understanding that honest differences of opinions will often lead to better outcomes. Executives should feel empowered to push back when they disagree with statements made by board members. The CEO and the board members must possess the requisite self-awareness not to monopolize limited board time. The board chair, both in how she publicly runs the meeting and in her private conversations with the CEO and the board members, must intentionally manage and gently provide counsel when boardroom behavior goes off course. The goal is to encourage board input and allow each board member an opportunity to provide oversight while at the same time preserving the sense of partnership and trust between and among the board and leadership team.

One strategy for the board and CEO to handle disagreement productively is to respond to dissent with a spirit of inquiry. This allows the CEO to ask for clarification or examples to spur a healthy dialogue. If the board is deeply divided, one option is to postpone the decision to allow time to gather more facts, to circle back to those who might not yet be on board, or to recommend to the board chair that a task force be created to come to an agreement and make a recommendation to the board. It also provides the CEO with additional time to discern whether the dissenter(s) may have made valid points. An organization is not well served if the dissension in the room is ignored. Disagreement needs to be brought out in the open, expressed sensitively, and addressed thoughtfully. When possible, the board chair should focus on the commonalities as well as the differences, ensuring that everyone is provided with an opportunity to speak and be heard at the end of the day.

Whether it is increased competition, disruption within an industry, or changing consumer preferences, virtually every organization is being forced to evolve at an increasingly faster rate. This may mean that an organization will need to become nimbler as it changes course, makes a significant investment in technology, closes a program, or seeks new revenue streams. This often requires the CEO and his team, working in partnership with the board, to recommend and implement disruptive change, which may result in layoffs or impacted stakeholders attempting to resist or raise concern. For the organization to move forward during these moments of disruptive change, it is imperative that an honest and transparent dialogue occurs and that the board communicates as one voice that they are supportive of the decisions of the CEO and the board once they are made.

CHAPTER 21

The Board in
Time of Crisis

One of the roles of the board is to make sure that processes are in place to prepare them for whatever adversity comes its way. A recent study found that within a six-year time frame, 69 percent of companies experienced at least one crisis.[29] Adversity comes in many forms. A natural disaster hits your community, your information technology systems are attacked, the stock market crashes, your CEO takes another job or suffers a heart attack, your organization is splattered across the front page of the newspaper, a major funding stream is lost, or a reputational scandal occurs. In times of crisis, an effective and prepared board can be the difference in whether an organization survives.

My wife and I own a condominium along the Gulf Coast of Texas in an eight-story high-rise. We share ownership with 111 other owners. Our building, along with numerous other similar high-rise condominiums, was severely damaged by Hurricane Harvey. As fractional owners of the common areas, we owners are collectively governed by a homeowners association board of directors, whom we empower to make decisions on our behalf. Every year at our annual meeting, the owners get together to vote on who we want to represent us on this board.

Immediately before Harvey made landfall, the board engaged in numerous conference calls and made the difficult decision to commit a significant amount of the individual condominium owners' resources to hire a company that specializes in disaster-recovery services. This allowed the condominium association to preposition assets so that immediately after the hurricane hit, it could bring in a team of people to limit any further damage, prevent mold from spreading, and create a roadmap for eventual recovery. The association made this decision not knowing if insurance would ultimately cover this cost or whether their efforts would ultimately prove successful or even be needed.

What the association had in its favor was that it had crafted an outstanding board. One of the six members had significant risk-management experience and was previously involved in a similar situation. Another member possessed substantial construction-related experience. The remainder possessed decades of leadership experience and were comfortable making big decisions. While they didn't immediately agree on a specific course of action, they had previously developed trust among one another so that they could talk through the difficult situation facing them and ultimately come to a solution.

Their quick decisive action minimized the damage to our entire building, and life returned to semi-normal within eight or so months. Other condominium associations were not so fortunate. For a variety of reasons, their boards did not act quickly and often could not agree on a plan of action. As a result, several other high-rise condominiums close by suffered significant mold damage, which required entire buildings to be gutted. It took more than four years for other condominiums located along the Gulf Coast to rebuild and reopen, with each unit owner typically incurring an emergency assessment of over $100,000 to cover the uninsured extra costs. In times of crisis, good boards matter.

In another situation, the board of a small private university was asleep at the wheel. The president of the university enjoyed a long tenure and over the years, the board had slowly but surely become his rubber stamp. What the board and president missed was that its historical financial engine was rapidly deteriorating and that the college was no longer competitive in its market. It was apparent, after the fact, that the previous board provided little oversight in holding the president accountable. After the president retired, the new president and current board unexpectedly were forced to devote the first several years to damage control. By necessity, they scrambled to create a strategy of survival before being able to implement a forward-looking vision for the future.

CHAPTER 22

Bet-the-Organization Decisions

There are times in an organization's life when bet-the-organization decisions simply need to be made. What worked for the organization in the past is simply no longer viable. Technology may have disrupted its business model. Maybe the product or service it provides is no longer wanted by consumers. Changes in the law may have decreased its revenue base. There is an opportunity to merge with a similar mission organization. If the board and CEO don't proactively address these situations, the organization will quickly become a shell of its former self. The art of governance demands that the board and CEO proactively identify and address the elephant(s) in the room. It necessitates that the board continually be educated about the changing dynamic of the external forces and be a proactive participant in crafting a future strategy around what the organization has a passion for and what it can be best at. The board should then create an economically sustainable model.

The form of the decision-making process will depend on the issue, the size and sophistication of the board, the board's culture, and the skill sets of the CEO. A board and CEO may be able to simply discuss, decide, and move on. In other situations, it may be helpful to engage a consultant to lead the conversation. At times, it is useful for the board to hear from an outside expert. Alternatively, the board chair and CEO may decide to create a subcommittee tasked to engage in a deep dive with the CEO and her team and bring a recommendation back to the board.

On three occasions during my twenty-three-year tenure as CEO, I asked the board chair, as part of a board-staff strategic analysis, to create a subcommittee of several of the more respected board members to work with senior staff to conduct a deep dive into a particular issue that we were wrestling with. These were situations that would have substantial implications—programmatic, financial, and reputational—for the organization going forward. One issue involved exiting the Medicaid-funded skilled-nursing-home line of business because, due to funding cuts, we were simply unable to continue to provide quality services without going bankrupt. On another occasion, we involved key members of our board to work with a consultant to consider changing our brand. On a third occasion, we wrestled with whether we should sell our upscale retirement communities, which could potentially result in the elimination of our organization's $60 million debt and create a $40 million endowment to help fund our larger and more-focused children's mission of breaking the cycle of child abuse.

While it took a significant amount of coordination and education of board members, at the end of the day, it was the right approach. Board members who might not be comfortable with change tend to be somewhat skeptical when hearing from the CEO about the need for such a big pivot. While they may trust the CEO, they may have difficulty initially accepting such a big change. There is comfort in knowing that board members whose professional acumen they trust are also supportive.

CHAPTER 23

The Art of Managing a Difficult Board Member

The CEO will, on occasion, experience a difficult board member. During my tenure, I have been blessed to have worked with and for at least ninety bosses. While most were outstanding, dedicated servants who functioned as a true team, on occasion, an issue needed addressing. For example, a board member and I initially held a difference of opinion on what should be the appropriate strategic plan going forward. Once, I endured a board member who, in his day job, served as president of a company whose own board had developed such a negative culture of blame and fear that he assumed that was how all boards operated. Another board member became close friends with a disgruntled staff member and initially believed his side of the story. A litigator by trade would utilize her excellent cross-examination skills to find holes in staff reports. These situations, while they required my attention, could be managed because of the trust that had been established in our individual and collective relationships.

Collectively, the board can fire the CEO. However, this is not a reciprocal option for the CEO. The CEO, working with the board, does, however, have several arrows in her respective quiver. Best practices dictate  that the board periodically reviews itself as a whole and that each board member also is reviewed by the board for her effectiveness. This allows the board chair to receive feedback on how to improve processes and meetings going forward. Many boards will also complete a brief survey after each meeting. What went well? What could be improved? Other boards have a policy that allows them to remove a board member who misses two or more consecutive meetings. While this is often unenforced, it is one lever at a board chair's disposal. At a minimum, it provides a mechanism for an honest conversation.

Well-governed boards will also evaluate individual board members who are eligible for reappointment to serve another term. This provides objective data for the governance committee or board to determine whether it is in the organization's interest for the board member to be reappointed. While boards are hesitant to not reappoint an existing board member, it may provide an opportunity for a board chair or governance-committee chair to have a productive conversation with the less-than-stellar performing board member, which may lead her to the conclusion that maybe her time and passion is best suited elsewhere.

I am aware of one board that has abolished term limits and has instead instituted term reviews. When a board member's term expires, the board chair and CEO will engage in a conversation with that board member to discuss the anticipated value-add of this board member going forward. Conversations center on what this board member has contributed in the past, the evolving organizational needs, any professional or time commitment changes that have occurred recently that might have an impact going forward, and whether there is a continuing board fit. It allows both parties to collectively opt out. In a high-functioning, healthy environment, this may increasingly become a best practice, especially if combined with some sort of outside term limits, for example, three or four three-year terms.

When a disagreement over strategy arises, arguing about facts typically results in one or both sides digging in and doubling down. A better strategy is for the CEO to utilize her emotional intelligence to understand why she and this specific board member don't share the same perspective. This is done by first building a relationship of trust and then using open-ended questions to understand the other person's values and perspective. Usually, each participant discovers a deepening empathy for the other's perspective as they attempt to stand in the other's shoes. Based on individual life experiences and the information the participants possess, each perspective is often rational. The goal is to agree with aspects of the opposite perspective as well as add new information to the conversation so that on her own, your colleague—and possibly you—can come to a different or at least more-nuanced conclusion.

When there is a strong relationship between the board chair and the CEO, there are times that it may be appropriate for the CEO to give the board chair a heads-up on a potential situation before it gets out of hand.

In the previous example involving the tendency of an attorney to go into cross-examination mode, I quietly gave the board chair a heads-up that there was an occasion or two after a board meeting that I would need to do damage control with a staff member who was offended by the style of questioning. This allowed the board chair to jump in on occasion and phrase questions in a softer manner. The attorney, because she possessed deep emotional intelligence, caught on and adjusted her style.

A mentor of mine jokingly gave me this advice: "The trick is to outlive a few of your board members." Just as the art and science of selecting the right CEO are imperfect at best, the art and science of choosing the right board members will never be perfect. Each board member brings different life experiences, and it is the CEO and the board chair's role to manage and adjust to the ever-changing landscape. It is also helpful to have a few trusted friends and family outside of the organization to let off steam on occasion while keeping a sense of humor about it all.

CHAPTER 24

The Art of Setting an Effective Agenda

One common complaint from board members is the amount of time boards must devote to passively receiving information. A lot of time is spent listening to management reports, reviewing financials, approving routine resolutions, and hearing committee reports. As a result, there is less than an ideal amount of time available to engage the CEO and his team on strategic issues of vital importance to the organization. A board member may even quietly question whether the CEO is purposefully keeping the board at arm's length. Or this may be how the board has always operated, meaning the current board chair assumes this is good governance.

Boards can have an enormous impact on what is and is not placed on their agenda. The art of designing a board agenda is to intentionally craft each moment so that the limited board time enhances the board members' knowledge, builds trust and relationships, and creates an environment that facilitates robust, strategic dialogue. The goal is to create an environment where the board serves as the CEO's highly engaged brain trust, which, in addition to fulfilling its various fiduciary responsibilities, provides invaluable feedback and guidance on critical issues that tie directly to the mission of the organization.

For a board to add value, each board member must not only be passionate about the mission but also believe that her time and talents are wisely utilized. Board members understand that a certain amount of time must be devoted to traditional governance functions such as reviewing financial statements, evaluating the CEO, and meeting with auditors. However, this alone is not enough. Board members crave to make a difference. A best practice is that every board agenda be crafted with the intention that at least half of each board meeting be devoted to the board and CEO engaged in a structured forward-looking dialogue that ties directly back to the mission and vision of the organization. Conversations are designed to be less of the CEO instructing the board about where the organization should head and more about creating an environment that allows each board member to effectively utilize his or her unique gifts.

Board members often don't realize their power of influence as they engage in appropriately structured dialogue with the CEO and senior staff. On numerous occasions, I have witnessed a board member make a comment that seemingly didn't make much of an impact at the time with other board members or senior leadership. However, later—often at a subsequent staff meeting—this comment spurred the senior leadership to further reflect, resulting in a healthy conversation that ultimately led to a more robust strategy going forward.

I currently serve as the chair of two boards of directors. One is an 800-million-dollar charitable foundation. The other is a multi-media international mission organization with offices in thirty-six countries. In both organizations, the CEO and I have instituted a practice where at least twice a year the board and senior leadership team engages in a deep dive into a topic or topics that could impact the future mission of the organization. First, the board is educated on the nuances of the topic and why it is important. Second, the board will often be broken up into small groups to continue the discussion with a senior staff member. And finally, each small group will report to the whole group, with further conversation coming from the entire board and leadership team as to what direction the organization should take.

For the board and the CEO to be aligned, both must understand that the organization's mission is their only reason for coming together and then act accordingly. For example, if a school district or charter school has set as its mission that all children, regardless of their socioeconomic or other backgrounds, will achieve at high levels, then as a team, the board and the CEO will follow through with a comprehensive strategy that is laser focused on closing the various achievement gaps. This clarity will be communicated not only in its core beliefs and strategic plan but also by how the board agenda is structured. The right board agenda will include a discussion on measurable results that tie back to its mission; an evaluation process based on how effectively the CEO has achieved the stated, measurable goals; a fiscally responsible budget that is aligned with its mission; and other appropriate, monitored data. The board will use this information to work collaboratively with the CEO to drive continuous improvement.

On occasion, specific issues will need to be teed up. Perhaps an outside industry expert will be brought in to educate and stimulate discussion or a consultant will be asked to lead a conversation about a specific elephant in the room. Effective strategic dialogue allows board members to lead with questions on topics that have been on their minds and for the CEO and the board to have a robust conversation. This leads to a board culture that embraces critical thinking and pushes the CEO and senior leadership team to view issues from a different perspective, which in turn leads to further internal robust, strategic discussions.

Setting the agenda is a shared responsibility between the board, the chair, and the CEO. During the latter part of my tenure as CEO, we utilized a uniform agenda format for each of our quarterly board meetings to provide consistency from meeting to meeting. Each quarter, we provided the board with a financial analysis that looked both backward and forward. More important, we spent at least half of our time engaging the board in an ongoing strategic dialogue. Each quarter, the board was also provided with an updated risk/rewards matrix that categorized our various ongoing initiatives as well as any new opportunities that may have arisen in the current quarter. This allowed for continuity of conversation, provided a mechanism for the board and staff to discuss vis-à-vis the backdrop of a risk/reward perspective, and gave the board a snapshot of all new potential opportunities. This naturally led to dialogue around capacity and mission.

We also met once or twice a year at one of our program sites. It allowed board members to do a deeper dive into a specific program as they met local staff and clients and asked specific questions about such things as staffing patterns, programmatic outcomes, various challenges, and opportunities. It made our subsequent conversation about the organization's financials real as board members connected the dots back to the programs. It enhanced their passion for the mission as they observed firsthand the impact that the organization's work had on the community. A board member's presence at a program site also enhances the job satisfaction of the local staff as they share their work with pride.

One national board that I chair holds an annual two-day retreat in a location outside of its corporate office. This allows time for more strategic discussions. More important, it allows us to have a working lunch with key customers as well as two private dinners with board members and senior staff. Because we are a national board, this is often the only time to get to know one another, as the other three meetings a year we typically quickly fly in and out with only a working breakfast and lunch together. Recently, the CEO and I decided to hold one of our quarterly board meetings via a conference call, with the understanding that the subsequent board meeting would be conducted over two days. This saved board members travel time and now allows the board and staff to conduct a deeper strategic dive twice a year.

Paying attention to how the boardroom is laid out can also influence the culture of the governance process. In one organization, the CEO and Chief Financial Officer (CFO) traditionally stood in front of the room at a podium as they addressed the board. The senior staff would sit quietly behind the board members to observe. The CEO and CFO would give their presentation, and the board would ask questions. While well-meaning, this layout unintentionally created an us-versus-them feeling. Because their organization was currently very stable and both the leadership team and board extremely talented, the board chair and CEO decided to change the format by having four key staff leaders sit at the board table; this encouraged more of a round-table dialogue as opposed to an inquisition. This minor change in the room setup changed the entire tone of the conversations and added to the underlying sentiment that the leadership team and the board are truly one team.

It is the responsibility of the CEO and the board chair to make sure that the board gets the right information. Here are some important questions to ask:

- Is the board receiving relevant information, such as data on the industry, changes in the external environment, or data on employee engagement?

- Are outside experts on occasion brought in to educate the board on the state of the industry, governance best practices, or the impact of technology?

* Is the format of the agenda consistently designed from one meeting to the next to provide continuity of strategic discussion?

* Is the board receiving too much or not enough information?

Again, this is where an experienced board chair with emotional intelligence can work closely with the CEO to ensure that the board is receiving what it needs.

Unless a CEO has also served as a board member of another organization, she can fail to appreciate how difficult it is for board members to recall the specifics of board discussion from one meeting to the next. The art of keeping the board involved in ongoing strategic conversation includes some level of strategic review at each meeting. It may also mean emailing the board a mid-quarter organizational update. It may mean the CEO talks to each board member between board meetings. This intentional consistency in agenda building and strategic discussion allows the CEO to educate how new plans and opportunities are, in fact, building blocks to executing the agreed-upon strategic plan. It also provides board members with the opportunity to provide counsel at each step.

An effective board will also carve out time at every board meeting to meet in executive session, first with the CEO and subsequently without the CEO. Healthy boards tend to spend most of the time engaged in conversation with the CEO present. They may do this, for example, to allow the CEO or board members the opportunity to address concerns they do not feel comfortable bringing up in front of other senior staff. An effective board chair will also discern when the board should meet alone. For a variety of reasons—some healthy and some not—some boards feel most comfortable assessing the productivity of the board meeting, the direction the organization is heading, and/or the effectiveness of the CEO without the CEO being present. In situations like this, the board chair needs to circle back to the CEO either that day or the next to provide appropriate feedback and updates so that communication gaps do not develop.

CHAPTER 25

The Art of the CEO Serving the Board

In addition to leading the day-to-day operations of the organization, the CEO has two primary tasks as it relates to the board. The first is to assist the board chair and/or committee chairs as they work to accomplish their assigned tasks. Board members are often not compensated, and it is unrealistic to expect them to do clerical work. The CEO, or in larger organizations, a senior member of the leadership team, can assist the committee chair in fulfilling her role. A CEO can provide draft committee charters and suggest updates to the policy manual. A CEO can keep track of what may be missing as it relates to best practices and then alert the board chair or governance committee. It is the role of the CEO to ensure that the board chair and committee chairs have the necessary tools at their disposal so they can perform their role effectively. While many of the ultimate decisions will fall within the purview of the board, a strong CEO will proactively drive and subtly influence the process for the good of the organization.

The second task of the CEO as it relates to board governance relates to the art of leading. Boards often forget that CEOs have a myriad of bosses. Depending on the setting, this may include regulators, customers, parents, members, bankers, clients, bondholders, vendors, partners, donors, volunteers, government officials, local communities, unions, or politicians in addition to their more formal bosses, board members, who have diverse backgrounds, levels of expertise, and on occasion, agendas. Even worse, CEOs often forget this as well. Even when they acknowledge this reality, there are never enough hours in a day to effectively satisfy every constituency, and so CEOs are forced to delegate, prioritize, or take shortcuts.

On occasion, what happens is that the CEO places on the back burner the care and feeding of the board. Or she focuses on the more influential leaders of the board, ignoring the rest. A CEO has often built up enough credibility so that this strategy can work for a few quarters or even years. However, it almost always ends badly. New board members have no institutional memory of what the CEO did or did not do in the past. When quarterly numbers are missed or something bad happens, the reservoir of trust simply isn't deep enough for the new board and CEO to get through this together. *that's a lot!*

A simple rule of thumb is that a CEO should spend 15 to 20 percent of her time communicating with and developing relationships with the board. It is the CEO's responsibility to establish a relationship with every board member. This can include scheduled quarterly phone calls, social gatherings such as lunch or dinner, monthly email updates, and the development of systems so that both bad and good news are shared in a timely manner with the board. This allows the CEO to intuitively understand each board member's strengths, weaknesses, priorities, and goals.

Why is this important? If an organization is achieving its goals, this task may not rise to the top of the list. However, the success of an organization never follows a smooth, upward path. A recession, a mistake by your least-competent employee, a missed financial goal, a tragic incident, or a change in the external environment can test the relationship of the CEO with the best of boards. A CEO must establish a relationship of trust from the beginning. Again, it is like a good marriage, knowing that even in the best of relationships there will be rocky moments.

Several years ago, my organization was impacted by the simultaneous occurrence of a recession and a major hurricane. I needed to have a difficult conversation to request the board's approval to dip into our reserves to keep our programs operating at current levels. In grudgingly approving my request, one board member, using a gambling analogy, commented, "Kurt, you have garnered a lot of chips with the board, but you just used one today." Fortunately, over the years, I had intentionally collected a few. I instinctively knew, however, that my pocket had just become one chip lighter.

CHAPTER 26

Good to Great +
the Social Sectors

The Art of Strategic Planning

The art of strategic planning is evolving. Strategic planning is an area where many boards and CEOs experience their greatest frustration, as there is a lack of clarity as to their respective roles. As a result, CEOs become frustrated with boards that they believe are meddling in areas in which they should not be, while board members are also frustrated and feel marginalized in the process. The traditional method of strategic planning—setting in stone a five-year plan with specific action steps outlined under each major goal—is, in the eyes of many, no longer the best path forward. The future is simply too uncertain, ambiguous, and increasingly complex to effectively plan step-by-step this far into the future.

In this brave new world, an organization must define its purpose and mission with laserlike clarity while at the same time be increasingly flexible in creating its strategy to accomplish its very focused mission. Here are some questions to be wrestled with:

- **What specific purpose does our organization play in its community, nation, or world?**

- **What unique slice of a societal problem will our organization solve?**

- **What service can we uniquely provide that is our core reason for existing?**

- **What is the board's role?**

Best-in-class organizations know why they exist and then protect their core at any cost. Every decision can then be made by first asking the questions "Will this enhance our mission?" "How does this tie back to our purpose?" Having a clear purpose and mission is the foundation for everything else that follows. Engaged employees will better understand the organization and their own roles. It allows the board and CEO to focus on their clients' outcomes, which will drive better decision-making and allocation of assets. It allows organizations to make difficult decisions, knowing that they can't be all things to all people. It allows a board to possess a better understanding of what skill sets are necessary for a CEO to succeed.

Jim Collins, in his seminal book *Good to Great: Why Some Companies Make the Leap and Others Don't*,[30] as well as his follow-up work, *Good to Great and the Social Sectors: Why Business Thinking Is Not the Answer*,[31] written specifically for nonprofit organizational leaders, empirically demonstrates that organizations that are more focused will outperform those that are less focused. Strategic questions that every board should ask include Does the organization have a focused mission? Has it translated this mission into a rigorous yet flexible strategic plan? Once an organization's purpose is crystalized, the resulting strategy becomes increasingly clear.

After decades of attempting to serve virtually all who were in need as part of our mission to be the most comprehensive social service organization in the region, the organization in which I served as CEO developed laser-focused clarity around its new mission to break the cycle of child abuse. Embracing this focused mission allowed us to next tackle one of several elephants in the room: that we simply didn't have the capital to continue to be a major player in the residential senior services space going forward. It allowed us to address the fact that our brand was no longer effectively supporting our mission. Our enhanced clarity provided us with the ability to create new programs, acquire new talent, and create a research and advocacy division. It provided us the opportunity to tell our story in a new way to new audiences. It permitted us to say no when new opportunities didn't fit our laser-focused mission. It allowed us to be more impactful in a very specific, targeted need of the communities in which we served. It provided us with an opportunity to demonstrate our results with evidence-based and evidence-informed outcomes.

As we initially embarked on this collective journey, we hired a traditional strategic-planning consultant to help guide us into the future. This individual organized us into various work groups and drove a somewhat expensive fact-gathering process that unfortunately merely verified what we already knew. It quickly became apparent to our Chief Operating Officer and me that this cookie-cutter process didn't fit our organizational culture. Our senior leadership team was growing frustrated. We already knew the salient facts: Our balance sheet was too leveraged, the external environment in which we operated was changing dramatically, we no longer had a focused mission, and we had become a staid, 130-year-old organization in need of reinventing itself to remain relevant in the future.

What we had in our favor was a sophisticated board and a strong senior leadership team that trusted each other. We quickly decided to change course. We believed that it would be better if, instead of letting the consultant lead the process, we would personally lead the strategic dialogue. We focused first on what our organization could potentially be best-in-class at. In missional terms, the conversation revolved around where our organization could have the most impact in enhancing the communities we serve. We quickly realized that because we were unique in that we were a provider of both education and social services, we could be best-in-class within the state of Texas at breaking the cycle of child abuse. Once we agreed upon our clarity of purpose and mission, it became much easier to agree on how to address the remaining elephants in the room.

For an organization to outperform its peers, it must possess a core purpose that is simple and convincing. From my perspective, while staff should have a strong voice at the table, often taking the lead and presenting to the board with recommended draft language, this decision ultimately rests with the board. With this clarity, the CEO and her team will bring to the board a draft strategic plan that connects purpose with practice.

For most organizations, it is not a best practice for the board to take the lead in creating a strategic plan. If the CEO and her team are strong, they will come to the table with a process and possibly a draft initial framework for the board to provide input. The art of governance allows the board to play its critical role of being trusted advisers to enhance the collective strategic efforts via an intentional, continual forward-looking dialogue. Boards should ask questions such as these:

- What is our role in our community?

- Is the plan achievable?

- Where are the holes?

- What are the risks?

- Is there a need?

- Who is the competition?

- How will we fund the strategy?

- Is it sustainable?

- How will we know if we are successful?

- Do we have the right talent?

- How will we know if our employees are engaged?

- How will we measure the results?

- What is the relevant empirical data?

- Does the organization have the resources, expertise, and passion to accomplish its agreed-upon mission?

For a board to play a meaningful role in shaping strategy, it must first do the hard work of truly understanding the organization and the external environment in which it competes.

- What are the various financial levers that the organization has at its disposal?

- Who are its competitors?

- How is the changing environment impacting its ability to accomplish its mission?

- What are the specific organizational risks that board members should be cognizant of?

- Who are the key stakeholders?

Sadly, some boards simply don't have the expertise to add significant value to shaping the strategic plan because they don't fully understand the organization and its complexities. Recruiting appropriate board members and educating the board so that they can add value necessarily is a nonnegotiable shared responsibility of the CEO and the board.

CHAPTER 27

Strategic Planning—
A Deep Dive

Diving a little deeper, we see that many boards don't pay adequate attention to their organization's most valuable assets, typically their employees. How well an organization serves its clients is largely dependent on its employees. Most nonprofit organizations create strategic and community value primarily through their human capital. While most of this responsibility rests with the CEO and her team, from an organizational-risk perspective, it is the board's responsibility to provide oversight. Again, what gets placed on the agenda and asked about at the board level gets paid attention to at the staff level. This may include engaging in a robust dialogue on the organization's compensation philosophy, receiving data on employee retention, reviewing year-over-year results of employee satisfaction surveys, or monitoring websites such as Glass Door to see what employees are saying about the organization. Dialogue may ensue around topics such as these:

- Is the organization adapting to meet the needs of today's workforce?

- How well does the organization recruit, train, retain, and motivate its workforce?

- Is a hybrid work-from-home-or-office model appropriate for our organization?

- What is the culture of our organization?

- How do we know?

Of necessity, boards are also increasingly focused on understanding the organization's technology strengths and limitations.

- Does the organization have a sophisticated back-office platform that will allow it to effectively grow?

- How will technology potentially disrupt the organization's strategy?

- What are the risks and rewards of investing scarce resources in technology?

- Has the organization appropriately protected itself against various technology risks such as cyberattacks, information-security incidents, password theft, and service outages?

- Can a smaller organization survive if it doesn't possess the capital to invest in technology?

If the answer to the last question is no, does the board, working with the CEO, have a fiduciary responsibility to proactively seek out a suitable outside partner?

As a CEO, consultant, and board member, I have engaged in countless strategic-planning exercises. Some lasted only a few hours, but others went on for months. Some were led in house, while others involved high-priced consultants. Some resulted in meaningful organizational change while others led to a written plan that was soon forgotten. The science of strategic planning will differ among organizations and is beyond the scope of this book. The depth and breadth of any process will often be dependent on the life cycle of the organization.

- Does the organization currently have clarity of mission?

- Has the external environment or leadership team radically changed?

- Have new competitors or technology disrupted the business model?

The more important questions get to the art of strategic planning. The process needs to be designed in a manner that effectively allows the board and senior leadership team to wrestle with and confront the brutal facts.

- **Is the organization accomplishing its mission? How do we know?**

- **Do we have the financial model to be successful over the long term?**

- **Do we have the right people sitting around the table?**

- **What are the critical issues that we need to acknowledge and address?**

These critical issues will often dictate the scope and structure of the strategic-planning process. Such topics may include new competitors, insufficient capital, changes in funding patterns, outdated technology, a lack of appropriate talent, an inefficient governance model, and a less-than-robust fundraising strategy, to name a few.

No plan completely survives its initial implementation. Embedded within the board's governance model will be a continual flywheel of assessment and adaptation. An organization will fail intelligently as initiatives get tested, revised, and implemented. Organizations are increasingly learning by trial and error as they continually adjust to the needs of their clients and the marketplace. In this type of environment, three-year plans with ninety-day metrics to determine whether an organization is on track, coupled with an increasingly focused mission, are increasingly becoming best practice.

To ensure that the plan stays top of mind and relevant in the ever-changing external environment, I have adapted my approach to fit this new reality. First, the senior leadership team and the board must agree on what they want to accomplish. What is their core purpose for existing? Before an organization can move on, there must be clarity to its purpose. Knowing that it is virtually impossible to plan five years out, the next step is for the organization to determine what three to five goals must be accomplished during the next three years to achieve this purpose, its core mission. Then, to create momentum and excitement in the organization, it must determine what one goal must be accomplished within the next twelve months to demonstrate that the organization is on track to achieve its stated mission. Finally, leaders should plan out what three to five 90-day goals must be achieved for the organization to be on track to accomplish its one- and three-year goals. Forcing an organization to continually come back to the planning table to assess whether it has well executed its 90-day goals, and then set new 90-day goals based on past learnings and changes in the external environment, provides a rigor that will allow the entire organization to keep its focus on achieving its mission. It also allows a board to incentivize and track purposeful behavior as well as tell great stories as the organization achieves its stated purpose.[32]

Being increasingly flexible is also an acknowledgment that the world in which we operate is moving too fast to accurately predict what should be measured even, at times, in as short a period as the next twelve months. Throughout all levels of the organization, there is value in creating a detailed operational plan to ensure that every department has clarity in its specific role. We can agree that there continues to be value in creating yearly metrics. However, the board should possess the flexibility and willingness to occasionally move or change the goalposts midyear in response to external events that are outside the control of management. As a former colleague of mine likes to say, "We had to zig instead of zag."

In this new world, experimentation is encouraged and supported. Setting specific targets, even on an annual basis, is still important but may be less vital than establishing a general sense of direction that leads to long-term impact and value creation. This intuitive understanding has led some boards to change their incentive plan for executives to provide the board with more flexibility in rewarding (or not) the leadership team by undertaking a more global assessment of management's success for the year, as opposed to rigidly assessing the achievement of the metrics that were established and agreed upon at the beginning of the year. This is where the art of governance becomes more important than a rigid focus on the science of governance. If done thoughtfully, it will allow a board and CEO to become closer partners in achieving the organization's mission, will lessen the temptation to play various games to meet previously agreed upon metrics that no longer make sense, and will send the appropriate signal to the CEO and leadership team that their board has their back in this age of uncertainty.

Another role of the board is to insist that the organization measure its performance with outcomes that tie directly back to its mission. If, for example, reading at grade level is a more powerful predictor of lifelong health than virtually any other metric, an organization that serves children in the education, health care, and social services space should be laser-focused on achieving this objective among other relevant metrics. Knowing that it may be impossible for one organization to accomplish this goal alone, having such metrics may also lead to conversations with other key stakeholders. For example, a school district and a social service organization may find that a shared partnership is the most effective strategy to ensure that each child is provided with the opportunities necessary to succeed.

In a world of limited funding, organizations that can provide demonstrable results will be able to differentiate themselves and remain sustainable over the long term. It is the role of the board and the CEO to chart a strategy that can demonstrate that their programmatic results are evidence-based, or at a minimum, evidence-informed. For many organizations, this will mean moving away from exclusively telling feel-good stories about who they serve to providing both qualitative and quantitative evidence that their organization is worth a funder's time and investment.

If the board and senior leadership team are not always vigilant, mission creep can occur even among the most careful of organizations. Pressure to grow, the appeal of a new product line or service, an attempt to emulate a competitor's strategy, and the difficulty to say no can all lead to mission creep. Not long after my organization's mission became laser-focused, I approached the board with an opportunity to merge with another organization that, while it operated similar programs, did not possess the same clarity in mission that we had. My board rightly pushed back, asking questions such as these: "How does this further our agreed-upon mission?" "What would the opportunity costs be if we went forward?" "Do we currently have the capacity?" After additional due diligence and discussion, I acknowledged that they were right in not pursuing the merger, which allowed us to refocus our time and resources on more organic opportunities that fit squarely within our mission. My board, because it was a strong board comfortable with asking hard questions, was able to keep my ego in check as I recommended something that would have accomplished a secondary goal of expanding the organization but would have also resulted in mission drift.

Effective strategic planning is an ongoing process that never ends. The art of strategic planning demands that the board and the CEO create a consistent, well-designed process to facilitate ongoing strategic conversations that incorporate both external and internal realities. Strategic leadership is the art of the possible. While there will be times in an organization's life when the board and staff will need to embark on a more rigorous process, effective strategic planning is always ongoing. Intentional, continual strategic assessment and reassessment go hand in hand with the execution of strategy and measurement of outcomes.

CHAPTER 28

The Art of Creating an Effective Strategy Goes beyond the Board

Today's board, no matter how intelligent and experienced, is, at times, unable to see the entire big picture and understand the risks and nuances of the strategies being discussed during its quarterly meetings. This increasingly fast-moving, complex environment requires an organization to intentionally be nimble and its leaders to seek strategic counsel proactively from a host of outside stakeholders. An effective CEO and senior leadership team by necessity will intentionally create and utilize a web of networks to help inform strategy.

In my organization, this web included advocacy groups, trade associations, foundations, key program partners, lobbyists, state officials, top-level bureaucrats, volunteer leaders, and business-advisory groups. All contributed to our effectiveness as the organization continued to create and execute well on its vision and strategy. The *art* of governance required me, as CEO, to intentionally create opportunities for board members to become intertwined into our organization's unique web of stakeholders. To accomplish this goal, we invited industry experts to present to our board. We arranged for site visits so that board members could personally interact with program staff, clients, and volunteers. We scheduled educational lunches with leaders of our foundation partners for a board member to attend with the CEO. We asked leaders of state agencies, lobbyists, and state senators to meet with our board. We recruited board members from our web of stakeholders.

An international nonprofit organization that has offices throughout the world arranges for several board members to make site visits. Its CEO also recently initiated virtual site visits, where local program staff interact with and educate the entire board via Zoom. A foundation makes it a practice for its board and various committees to meet with experts in the investment world, key stakeholders, futurists in the foundation environment, executive compensation experts, and governance gurus, all to keep its talented board engaged and up to speed on the latest trends in this changing environment. Other strategies to weave an organization's web of networks into its governance model include sending board members to an industry conference or inviting a board member to testify at a legislative hearing.

CHAPTER 29

The Art of Change Management

On occasion, a new board member or a recently hired CEO will join the board and realize that the organization's governance model could be strengthened. Board meetings may consist of death-by-PowerPoint presentations, or the board may have become a rubber stamp for the CEO. On the other side of the coin, the board may inappropriately be meddling in the operations purview of management.

How does a new board member or CEO change an ineffective or dysfunctional board culture? All too often, a new board member or CEO will fail in the attempt if he moves too quickly or doesn't properly consider the group dynamics of an existing board. It is often a fool's errand to tell a board that their culture of doing business is inadequate and that you have a better way. The group will find a way to marginalize your efforts.

I served on a board that, due to a strong and successful CEO, had become, in my opinion, too passive in its governance responsibilities. We spent most of our time looking backward and, after the first couple of meetings, it appeared that no real board-level strategic discussions took place. I also discerned that several other newer board members possessed significant board expertise and seemed to be having a similar reaction as me. I would ask an occasional question about strategy or board process, often using the new-board-member card to slowly but surely plant seeds that others could pick up on. Fortunately, our talented CEO also realized that his current board was more sophisticated than past boards and was amenable to enhancing the governance process. He also understood that it was in the organization's interest to strengthen the board's culture so that collectively we could make a good decision about his replacement, as he planned to retire in a few years.

The art of managing a board suggests that it is in a new CEO's interest to first create relationships with board members before recommending substantive changes to the governance model. Too many CEOs come into the role believing that simply by the fact that they were hired by the board they have been empowered to immediately make changes. They forget that trust must come before partnership and that forging a bond of trust takes time. Newer CEOs will want to intentionally develop allies on the board who are likely to support needed governance enhancements. A new CEO will know that the board wants her to succeed or they wouldn't have hired her. However, many board members also have a connection to the past that the new CEO often does not. Even though the board knows that change is necessary and for the best, at times, the grieving process of leaving the past unintentionally causes a board member to act emotionally as opposed to intellectually. Board members simply want to get to know the new CEO first and understand her rationale for change before they are called upon to place their reputations on the line to support her recommendations.

I currently serve as a coach to a new CEO. Upon his arrival, he discovered that he had inherited a compliant, rubber-stamp board, some of whom continue to have social ties to the retired CEO. He questioned whether the board possessed the skill sets and acumen needed for today's world. Fortunately, he has twelve to twenty-four months to make the necessary strategic changes. He is taking time to intentionally develop relationships with board members. He has discovered that he has an ally in one of the more sophisticated, well-respected board members. Instead of trying to change everything at once, which will appear to be a repudiation of the popular retired CEO, he is methodically educating his board and introducing small aspects of change at each board meeting. During this period, he is also continuing to build trust with the veteran board members while simultaneously recruiting new board members who will be more open to changes in culture and governance. Because he has the requisite emotional intelligence to be an effective leader, which is why they hired him in the first place, he is quietly making significant progress that will have a lasting impact.

CHAPTER 30

Who Is a Nonprofit Board Accountable To?

A nother topic that effective boards wrestle with is the question of who they are accountable to. This is an especially difficult question for nonprofit organizations that have no shareholders but, rather, exist exclusively for the good of the community. The law is clear that a nonprofit's sole reason for existing is to serve its community by fulfilling its stated mission and purpose. This legal responsibility lies not with the CEO but with the board. It is the board's responsibility to ensure that the organization is acting in the best interest of the community or region in which it serves. It is also a good governance practice to demonstrate via measurable outcomes to its stakeholders that it is fulfilling its role.

Being organized as a nonprofit organization brings a host of advantages. Typically, the organization is tax exempt, supporters are provided tax deductions for their contributions, debt financing is often more readily available at a lower cost, and the organization can place its mission above all other priorities, including maximizing financial return. In exchange, the law demands that board members and the CEO place the interests of the organization ahead of their own personal or professional interests and make decisions that weigh the competing needs of its various stakeholders. It is also called upon to balance the short- and long-term impacts of its various decisions. And while financial considerations can and should be considered, it is just one of many competing interests that the board must wrestle with.

My previous organization recently had to appropriately wrestle with such a situation. The senior leadership team and board collectively decided to sell an independent living community that cared for the elderly poor. We no longer possessed the requisite expertise, and it simply did not fit within our more focused mission. We intuitively knew, however, that we had a responsibility to other stakeholders that went beyond our ability to maximize profits from the sale of the asset. Collectively, we agreed that any sale must be a win-win for the residents, employees, local community, and last, our organization. This shared understanding provided management with the flexibility to seek buyers who would continue to operate this community for those who couldn't afford to pay, evaluate potential purchasers based on the quality of services they delivered, designate a portion of the proceeds to create an endowment that would continue to support the elderly in this particular community, and be empowered to say no to the highest bidder if it did not meet our criteria. Publicly sharing with everyone our stated criteria allowed us to complete this transaction with very little negative feedback from the residents, employees, or community.

On occasion, board members are tempted to place their self-interests ahead of the organization on whose board they serve. I recently consulted with a CEO who was frustrated because one of his board members insisted that the organization's endowment be invested with his employer's investment firm. He was annoyed that the CEO even mentioned the need to circulate a request for proposal to seek other interested applicants, even though the board member's firm did not have previous experience in managing endowments of nonprofit organizations. A board member should never place a CEO in such an awkward and potentially ethically compromising position. In such a situation, other members of the board must support the CEO and make it clear that this type of behavior is unacceptable and a violation of their fiduciary obligations.

Another area in which nonprofit organizations often struggle is in the realm of mergers and acquisitions. In the for-profit world, engaging in a merger or being acquired by another company offers the possibility of a significant payout for its founders, investors, and other equity holders. There is a very clear legal standard that the interests of the shareholders must come first. While we have all witnessed that this cut-and-dried approach has potential future negative ramifications for customers or employees, it does provide a roadmap for both boards as they determine, from a fiduciary lens, whether such a transaction makes sense for their companies.

Within the nonprofit world, there is no such similar clarity. Here are some questions that nonprofit boards wrestle with when considering mergers or acquisitions:

+ Will this enhance our ability to achieve our mission?

+ How will this impact the community?

+ What are the cultural impediments?

+ Will there be synergy between the two organizations?

+ Which organization will be viewed as the winner?

+ Which CEO will lose his or her position?

+ Will the community be upset if we make this decision?

+ Will I lose my board seat?

+ Can we as an organization survive if we don't find a suitable partner?

Nonprofit mergers and acquisitions are incredibly difficult to consummate, as executives and board members often receive nothing in return and will likely lose their position, prestige, and even monetary rewards for their efforts to strategically position their organization to enjoy enhanced missional impact and/or efficiencies of scale via a merger or acquisition. Either consciously or subconsciously, boards often choose the easier course of action by voting against such a marriage and continuing to muddle along alone, even if the organization remains underfunded or less than successful.

These fears are real and have proven to be huge barriers to nonprofit organizations that seek to enhance their impact via such a strategy. The art of governance provides us with an appropriate framework to overcome these informal barriers. The first rule is that board members and the CEO have a responsibility to place the mission and purpose of their organization first. In considering a merger or acquisition, some primary questions must be wrestled with:

+ Will a merger or acquisition enhance the long-term impact on the mission of the organization?

+ What strategic decision will best serve the community?

- What are the potential risks?

- Will one plus one ultimately equal three?

Once these questions are answered, the next step is for both organizations to follow the golden rule as it cares for those impacted by the change.[33] This may mean considering providing some sort of payout or consulting agreement to a departing CEO or other employees. It may mean creating a new board where some, but maybe not all, board members will be asked to continue to serve. It may mean that the organization that is closing its home office commits to continuing to have a significant presence in the community to minimize the pain to that community.

The art of governance also provides opportunities for two organizations to "date" before deciding to take the plunge. Collaborative efforts such as sharing back-office resources, joint ventures, fundraising, and other kinds of programmatic partnerships can be a good first step. As the operating environment in which organizations serve continues to become more complex, the simple reality is that increasingly, less-than-adequately capitalized and smaller nonprofit organizations may have to wrestle with these difficult decisions. Often the question for a board comes down to this: Does it want to run the risk of becoming a zombie organization that never fulfills its potential? Or is it willing to place its individual and collective self-interest on the back burner, knowing that its only purpose is to serve society?

CHAPTER 31

The Art of Holding the CEO Accountable

Understanding that a board's sole responsibility is one of service to society necessitates that the CEO be held accountable. This duty is often one of the board's most difficult jobs. Often a board member has a friendship with the individual he is to hold responsible. No board member enjoys asking difficult questions about a CEO's performance. In an age where every organization is placed under a microscope, a board must have mechanisms in place to hold the CEO accountable. A CEO and her team understand that there is a need for more accountability than in the past. Boards must realize that evaluating and measuring the CEO is one of their most important tasks.

The art (along with some science) of holding a CEO accountable is not all that difficult if the board is willing. The science aspect includes creating a system of checks and balances that are designed to produce warning signals before an organization is placed at risk. Here are some that may be included:

- Mutually agreed upon key performance indicators that typically provide consistent year-over-year measures as well as more focused CEO goals that may change year to year

- Annual executive-session conversation with the organization's auditors outside of the presence of the CEO

- Quarterly review of the expense account of the CEO and possibly the top officers

- Quarterly review of financial statements and investment results

The CEO and the board should annually agree to the appropriate organizational metrics because it is common wisdom that what gets measured gets managed. Boards should not be afraid to ask questions like these:

+ **Are we as an organization using the right metrics or key performance indicators?**

+ **Are these metrics and indicators well defined and quantifiable?**

+ **Do the metrics and indicators tie back to the strategic goals?**

+ **Should a portion of the CEO's compensation be tied to whether the organization achieves its goals?**

Many organizations are moving away from focusing on short-term results to the more difficult task of also measuring evidence-based and evidence-informed outcomes. How do we know that our work today will produce positive long-term outcomes? This journey will be worth the struggle when an organization can prove to its stakeholders and funders that not only is it serving well its clients today but it can also demonstrably prove that its communities will be better off in the future.

The art of measuring the work of the CEO is understanding that there are multiple dimensions to how a CEO and her team should be evaluated. While each organization will be unique, here are some common assessment themes that cross most organizational boundaries:

+ **The integrity and passion of the CEO**

+ **The CEO's ability to set strategy and achieve agreed-upon results**

+ **How the CEO builds and keeps talent**

+ **The CEO's ability to create a healthy organizational culture**

+ **Management of the organization's long-term financial health**

+ **If the organization is moving in the right direction**

- **How the CEO manages employee engagement**

- **The CEO's ability to manage the organization's unique set of stakeholders**

It also requires creating a culture that allows the board to engage in an honest, trust-filled, sensitive dialogue with the CEO.

A thoughtful board, as it designs an appropriate process to annually evaluate its CEO, will consider its unique context. To keep from having this annual event become merely a check-the-box task, it is helpful to use different approaches to evaluate the CEO, thus providing different perspectives and data points. In some years, a confidential 360 survey, completed by both board members and direct reports, may be appropriate. In other years, the chair of the board or personnel committee may decide to interview each board member, asking them to provide specific examples of the CEO's successes as well as areas in which he can improve. Or a board may decide to utilize a more traditional evaluation survey that ranks the CEO on a scale of one to five in various categories as well as provide opportunities for comments. Or the questions can be framed to promote a visioning exercise, where the board provides feedback as to where the organization is headed and the role that is expected of the CEO in the coming year.

The end goal is to receive useful feedback from various sources in a variety of methods that the board chair and/or committee chair can then confidentially aggregate and engage in an informed discussion with the CEO to discuss how he can continue to enhance his skill sets to benefit the organization. Making it a board custom to consistently provide feedback to the CEO provides a natural mechanism that doesn't feel punitive should performance issues arise that need addressing. This intentional feedback, coupled with a system to provide more informal feedback during and after each board meeting, will also promote continuous improvement and strengthen the board-CEO relationship. Best practices include engaging the CEO in a confidential conversation during an executive session as well as having the board chair circle back to the CEO after each meeting to share any concerns that may have arisen and, when appropriate, to compliment her for leading a productive board meeting.

Having these types of systems in place increases the likelihood of flagging any potential problems early. Human nature is such that if a leader is not held accountable, too often he becomes entitled. A CEO may justify padding his expense account because he believes that his board is underpaying him vis-à-vis his peers. Or a CEO retires on the job because he built this organization to where it is today and so he deserves to not have to work as hard as previously. In other situations, the organization has simply become too complex, and the current CEO may no longer have the appropriate skill sets to be effective. Or maybe it was simply a less-than-perfect hire by the board from day 1.

The art of holding a CEO accountable also includes understanding that every CEO will have shortcomings. Assuming the CEO's strengths more than make up for his weaknesses, the art of board governance is to harness this culture of trust that allows him to continue to develop as a leader. This may mean hiring a coach to develop his soft skills. In one situation, the board realized that their new CEO had excellent emotional intelligence and good intuitive skills. However, he lacked the experience to lead such a large organization. The board agreed that it would be in the organization's best interest for him to attend a Harvard Business School summer program for nonprofit leaders. This program was invaluable in teaching this CEO how to effectively lead his organization, manage his team of people, and better understand the financial intricacies of the organization. In another situation, we asked our newly minted CEO to work with a public speaking coach to assist him in becoming a more effective communicator.

CHAPTER 32

Integrity, Self-Care, and Blind Spots

The nonnegotiable baseline for any CEO is integrity. We regularly read or hear about the deserved removal of a CEO who had an inappropriate relationship with an employee, made an off-color comment, or otherwise embarrassed the organization. It is yet another reminder that we are living amid a cultural and technological sea change. Every public, and sometimes private, action will be scrutinized by stakeholders, media, donors, and employees. There is no longer a grace factor for generationally or regionally rooted excuses. Every CEO will be scrutinized for every public utterance of how he thinks or feels. Just as critical as how well the CEO drives strategy will be the perceived ethics of his actions.

The new rule, fair or not, is that CEOs must resist the temptation to make or even like inflammatory statements on social media. Understand that everything you say or do is available for public consumption. Off-color comments made in jest will be recorded and used against you. Know that a wide variety of stakeholders, including some who do not have your best interests at heart, will be scrutinizing your every technological footprint. Realize that virtually anyone can discover your net worth and where you and your family live. Resist the temptation to respond to internet trolls in moments of anger or frustration. If a response feels justified, consult first with a neutral third party, preferably someone with experience in this arena. Life as a CEO may not always be fair. It is, however, today's reality, and CEOs must adapt to be successful.

Unless one has served as a CEO, it is difficult to understand the accompanying burden of this responsibility. The CEO understands that if her organization doesn't deliver on its promises, employees may lose their jobs, which will in turn impact their families. One mistake by your least-competent employee can have a real-life negative impact on a client. A CEO wakes up every morning knowing that someone has offered an opinion about his organization in the press, on social media sites such as Glass Door or Twitter, or to a board member. The result is a 24/7/365 constant state of stress that needs to be intentionally managed.

Being a CEO can be a very lonely occupation. Every CEO must find a healthy way to manage this new reality. For me, this includes intentional daily rituals that center on keeping in God's Word, spending time with family, and exercising. It is also important emotionally to create safe places; to be able to engage in honest, open conversations without fear of being judged; and to know that your confidants are not afraid to question, challenge, confront, and comfort when appropriate. My confidants are my spouse and three trusted friends who also happen to be CEOs and so can relate and counsel with wisdom and empathy. For others, it is a trusted coach, pastor, or therapist. The board can and should play a supportive role. When appropriate, it should publicly and privately demonstrate that it has the CEO's back. It can offer to have the organization pay for a personal, confidential coach. It can privately provide counsel when it sees a CEO making a poor choice of words or actions. Maybe most important, it can create a culture of trust and support so that the CEO is aware and appreciative that she is not in this alone.

Experience suggests that three personality traits are good predictors of whether a CEO may ultimately fail. The first has to do with ethics and authenticity. If a CEO has a blind spot when it comes to acting with integrity, that individual will ultimately fail. Leaders cannot lead when employees and stakeholders don't want to follow, and a leader without integrity simply won't have followers. Integrity cannot be taught. If this is an issue, a board will necessarily have to act quickly to prevent the organization from being damaged. The second reason why CEOs are not successful in their role is the lack of a growth mindset. Unless a leader is constantly reinventing herself, ultimately, the world and the organization will surpass her skill sets. The third categories of leaders who are more likely to fail are those who possess a lack of self-awareness. They may have an inflated sense of their own skill sets. They may have risen to the top because of their technical skills and, as a result, minimized the importance of interpersonal relationships. They may simply lack sufficient emotional intelligence for this new role. This deficit can, on occasion, be corrected with appropriate coaching.

As a board member, one should continually assess whether your CEO possesses traits that could prevent the organization from achieving its full potential. It is part and parcel of the art of being a good board member.

CHAPTER 33

The Art of Retaining Your CEO

An overlooked aspect of the art of board governance is to create an environment where your talented CEO has no interest in leaving your organization. Every board must assume that its CEO is being tempted by inquiries offering greener pastures, more responsibility, new challenges, and increased compensation. If, as a board, you believe that your CEO acts decisively, is skilled at creating engagement among stakeholders and employees that produces results, adapts naturally to the changing external environment, and has integrity and passion for the organization's mission, one of the most important roles your board can play is to ensure that your CEO knows she is valued and properly cared for.

Board members, many of whom have never served in the role as a CEO, are simply not aware of how difficult the role can be. The relentless stress; the need to continually have difficult conversations with employees and stakeholders; the ambiguity in having to decide between two less-than-perfect choices; the homegoing at the end of the day, knowing that your tasks are not completed; the need to be available 24/7 to respond to the constant barrage of emails, texts, voicemails, Facebook Messenger, LinkedIn, and Twitter DM requests; balancing the demands of making a payroll versus adequately caring for your employees and clients all take a psychological toll on a CEO.

An effective board will intentionally care for its CEO. It will ask the CEO what is important to her, which may be a flexibility of schedule or the ability to occasionally work remotely. A board may agree to pay the membership dues at a local health club for the CEO and spouse. It may offer to pay for a personal coach. It may decide to, on occasion, provide the CEO with a sabbatical. It can create a policy that reimburses payment for spouse travel on appropriate business trips. Boards can reimburse the CEO for the cost of an annual physical. They can artfully craft a compensation package that is fair and meets the CEO's specific needs.

Maybe most important, individual board members and, more formally, the personnel committee and board chair can intentionally provide the CEO with encouragement and constructive feedback. Looking back on my career, it was the periodic heartfelt "Thank you" that most impacted my emotional health and desire to want to remain in the position of CEO. The recruitment of a good CEO does not end at her hire. It is a continual process and intricate dance that depends on a board being an encourager while simultaneously holding the CEO accountable.

CHAPTER 34

Knowing When It Is Time to Leave

Another role of being an effective board member is to know when leaving is best for the organization. The reasons for leaving are many. A board member may have accepted a new professional role, experienced changes in his family life or health, or no longer have the appropriate qualifications. I serve on a board on which a spouse of a community leader also served. To her credit, after several years of service, she realized that the complexity of the organization had overtaken her skill sets and that she was no longer effectively contributing as a board member. She voluntarily approached the CEO and the board chair and requested that she be allowed to resign from the board while also offering to continue her association with the organization as a volunteer and public supporter. She had the foresight to understand why the organization wanted her involvement. And while she had a passion for the organization, she was able to remove her ego from the decision-making process to do what was truly best.

In organizations that don't have board term limits, board members often stay past their useful board life. Term limits are, in my opinion, a best practice and serve a real purpose. Six, nine, or twelve years, depending on the nature and culture of the organization, is more than enough for an individual to add her unique value to an organization. Beyond a certain point, it is more likely that incremental value will be added by a new board member who can offer fresh experience, insight, youth, and diversity of thought as opposed to a board member who has been sitting at the table for decades.

The same is true for the CEO. Every five or so years, the board and CEO should engage in an open, trust-filled conversation as to whether this CEO remains the right person for this specific role going forward.

As a CEO, every few years, I quietly conducted a heartfelt inquiry as to whether I was still the best person for this role. I would ask my spouse and a handful of trusted confidants, including, but not limited to, a few trusted board members. The conversation was never about money, perks, or prestige. The art of governance centers the conversation solely around what is best for the organization, knowing that your healthy board will follow the golden rule in making sure that you are cared for if leaving is indeed best for the organization.

A couple of years ago, I prayerfully discerned that my time as CEO should come to an end. While the organization was achieving its goals, I was beginning to understand that my skill sets, while right for the organization today, were not necessarily the ones needed to lead this organization into the future. After prayer and intentional discernment, I reached out to my board chair and asked that he begin thinking about a succession plan, as I thought it best for the organization that I depart in approximately eighteen months. This gave the organization time to engage in an orderly leadership transition process. Because the board and senior staff enjoyed a relationship of mutual trust and respect, the organization continued to serve our clients and communities well during this transition period.

CHAPTER 35

The Art of Necessary Endings

The world is changing at a dramatic pace. The space in which our organizations operate is not the same as five years ago. Pandemics, remote office arrangements, inflationary pressures, and difficulty in recruiting and retaining qualified employees have become the norm. Funding streams shift, business opportunities arise, and technology continues to play an increasingly important role in the success of virtually every organization. The skill sets I needed to be successful when I was hired to be CEO twenty-three years ago are far different than what is required of CEOs today.

Necessary endings are a part of the fabric of our personal lives and vibrant organizations. Taking an organization to the next level can mean intentionally letting something or someone go. An organization, after reviewing the brutally honest facts, may conclude that it has become a jack of all trades and master of none. An organization may no longer have the capital and expertise to compete with larger for-profit competitors. To be successful, it will have to change the way it does business, enter new program lines, develop new partnerships, invest in a more sophisticated fundraising platform, replace existing talent with needed expertise, and/or bring on new board members with different skill sets.

Most CEOs can adapt to a changing environment. It is what made them successful as a CEO in the first place. They are self-reflective, are able and open to growth, and are secure in surrounding themselves with other smart people. During private conversations with trusted members of his board, a CEO should raise the question of whether he continues to be the right person to serve in this role. If the organization truly comes first, then the question is not what is best for the CEO but, rather, what is best for the organization.

Far too often, boards are also unwilling to engage in conversation about such a possibility. As the current owners of the organization, the board must periodically engage in honest conversations as to whether there continues to be a good fit between the needs of the organization and the talents of the CEO. Here are some examples of questions to ask:

+ **Has the external environment dramatically changed?**

+ **Is the CEO continuing to achieve the agreed-upon goals and metrics?**

+ **Does the CEO have the support of the employees and key stakeholders?**

+ **Can the CEO adapt?**

+ **How difficult would it be to find an outstanding replacement?**[34]

Unless a framework for objective analysis is used, this can be an uncomfortable conversation. My counsel is to always begin with these questions:

+ **What is best for the organization?**

+ **What are the risks to the organization of not doing anything?**

+ **What are the risks of making a change?**

This allows the board to take the personality or relationships out of the equation. Endings are part of the everyday experiences of life, and organizations are no different. A healthy board and CEO will normalize this reality and their approach to assessing their unique situation—be it aspects of their strategy or whether they have the right talents to successfully compete in today's environment.

If the board decides that a change of leadership is necessary, and assuming this is not a situation that involves unethical behavior, the next question a board must wrestle with is—in following the golden rule—How does the organization compassionately care for the soon-to-be-departing CEO? This includes getting prepared to have a difficult conversation. Henry Cloud, in his book *Necessary Endings: The Employees, Businesses, and Relationships That All of Us Have to Give Up in Order to Move Forward,* encourages the communicator of bad news to begin with the end in mind. What do you want the result to be? It may be clarity that a decision has been made and then an outline of the reasons why. The board may want to make sure that the outgoing CEO hears that he added great value during his time. The most effective conversations are those that incorporate both truth and care.[35] Like everyone, I have dreaded these types of conversations and often lost sleep the evening or week before. What I have discovered, however, is that when my difficult conversation was both clear and compassionate, the outcome often became as positive as it could be, given the circumstances.

In some situations, an employment contract will state the financial ramifications of a departure. Or the board may need to determine what is an appropriate and fair severance package, knowing that it is often difficult for a CEO to quickly find an equivalent employment opportunity. And while a fair severance package is an appropriate starting point, following the golden rule requires a board to go beyond monetary compensation. To the extent possible, unless there have been legal or ethics violations, a board will want to go beyond the call of duty to provide outplacement services, professional coaching, a positive press release, and a going-away party for the outgoing CEO. All are intended to appropriately honor someone who gave much of his life to the organization and to demonstrate to employees and stakeholders that the board and organization are indeed caring.

CHAPTER 36

The Art of Succession Planning

The greatest value a board can add to its organization is to hire and retain the right CEO. As the first step for fiduciaries, no matter what the corporate structure or size they serve, it is essential that the board and current CEO intentionally engage in ongoing succession planning. At its core, the goal of succession planning is to have in place a continual mechanism for a sound transition to sustain the mission of the organization going forward.

For a host of reasons, succession planning is a topic that is often ignored. The board is lulled into thinking that its current CEO will be around for another decade. It is often difficult to engage a high-performing CEO in this discussion, as she isn't planning on leaving anytime soon. The CEO may not trust the board to engage in an honest conversation about his future or potential successors. The art of good governance dictates that a regular cadence should be implemented on the topic of succession planning to help minimize the sensitivities surrounding this delicate topic.

There are three primary components to the art of succession planning. First, most organizations are of the size that it is a best practice for the board and CEO to intentionally groom one or two potential future internal candidates. I am chagrined at how many CEOs of organizations with one hundred, three hundred, seven hundred, and even over one thousand employees believe that no one in the organization is qualified to succeed them. If this is the case, both the CEO and the board have failed in one of their primary duties. Either the CEO is not recruiting and retaining the right people for her leadership team or members of her team are not receiving the appropriate ongoing coaching and development.

The art of governance dictates that succession planning should be a topic that is openly discussed by the board and CEO and that this is a primary responsibility of both the board and the CEO. Anecdotally, I have found that the time the board spends on succession planning is also proportional to the time that the CEO and his direct reports spend on succession planning, at all levels of the organization. It does not mean that the CEO gets to select his successor, nor will the board necessarily select an internally groomed candidate. However, having a defined, intentional succession process greatly reduces the risk of hiring a CEO who fails when the time comes. It can also serve as a retention strategy, as qualified internal candidates can envision a future within the organization. On two boards that I serve on, ongoing succession planning has been added to the written charter of a specific committee. This committee works closely with the CEO in designing a leadership development plan for its potential internal candidates. Best-in-class boards will also engage in a confidential conversation with the CEO as to what potential external candidates the board should reach out to when the time comes.

A second corollary is to ensure that if the CEO were to be hit by a bus or unexpectedly depart, then the board would have a plan in place for who can step in as interim CEO. Ideally, it is an internal executive. If necessary, it could potentially be a qualified board member or outsider. If there is a qualified internal candidate, a best practice is to name that individual quickly, either on an interim or permanent basis. This sends an immediate message to stakeholders and employees that the board is engaged and that the agreed-upon strategy will continue.

The third component is the selection process itself. In many situations, the board is given the luxury of time in selecting the next CEO. Assuming there is a relationship of trust that has been built up between the CEO and the board, the CEO will be comfortable signaling to the board that in, say, six months or two years, he plans to depart. This allows time for the board to make a variety of decisions. Are there appropriate internal candidates that they should begin to intentionally assess? Should these internal candidates be given new responsibilities to gain further experience? Who will lead the process? The entire board, a board succession planning committee, or the personnel committee? Is there a need for the board to recruit outside candidates? Should the board hire a search firm to guide the process?

On one board that I serve on, we began this conversation with the new CEO in his first year to naturally include him in this process. The board made it very clear that we have great respect for him, that he is an outstanding CEO, and that we will work hard to retain him. We also made it an annual conversation regarding who could succeed him in an emergency, and we engaged in an annual dialogue regarding potential internal candidates and what opportunities the organization could provide to further develop the skill sets of those candidates. Finally, we reminded him of the importance, if possible, of giving the board a one- to two-year lead time when he does consider moving on.

In another organization, the CEO had enough trust with his board to share with them that he planned to step aside within the next five years. During this time, the board and he intentionally created a development plan for the internal candidate. The plan included that the internal candidate would assume the title of president two years prior to the CEO's departure. During those two years, the internal candidate would continue to assume additional responsibilities. While no promises were made, this promotion sent a clear message to the entire organization that the board was taking succession planning seriously. It also freed up the CEO to focus on what he did best, which was to create new markets that would have an even greater impact going forward.

Research performed by the University of South Carolina found that CEO succession is most likely to fail if the board has not previously intentionally prepared for a smooth succession.[36] The research also increasingly demonstrates that, when possible, an organization should groom and select an internal candidate—unless the organization needs a strategic pivot.[37] The right internal candidate is more likely to succeed in that she typically has already built credibility within the leadership team and other stakeholders. There is an already-earned trust when the new CEO makes necessary difficult decisions. An internally selected CEO also understands the culture, including the board, and so there is less risk of failure when an organization pivots from one CEO to the next.

There are, of course, times when an organization must look outside for its next leader. The organization may be too small to have an appropriate internal candidate. The organization is simply at a point in history where a significant change in strategy or culture is necessary. Or the organization hasn't previously fulfilled its fiduciary role to appropriately prepare an internal candidate or candidates.

CHAPTER 37

Understanding the
What before the *Who*

It is tempting for a board to move quickly to the question of *who* would be best suited for the role of CEO. The conversation may quickly turn to the appropriateness of an internal candidate. The current CEO will also most likely have a strong opinion as to who is or is not the best candidate. Subconsciously, he may favor his protégé or a candidate who is most like him, even though the world has changed dramatically since he first became CEO. Before a board begins talking about the *who*, the board chair or designated committee must create a process that allows the board and possibly the senior leadership team to discuss *what* they are looking for in the next CEO.

This is often done by bringing in a consultant or a respected board member to interview each board member, the outgoing CEO, and selected members of the senior leadership team. The goal is to understand the current and future requirements of this role. Going deeper, the conversation then centers around what two or three capabilities are critical to the future success of the organization. This process acknowledges that, as the external environment has evolved, the qualities of the current CEO may not necessarily be the capabilities that are needed in the next CEO.[38]

This process allows for everyone to have input and will result in an in-depth dialogue as to the *what* before the conversation turns to the *who*. For example, one board initially wrestled with whether the next CEO for a large nonprofit organization needed to have previous nonprofit experience or if it was acceptable—or even preferable—for the candidate to have complex business experience in the for-profit world. In another example, the board of a historically Methodist organization that operates government-funded programs in a southeastern state that has very few citizens who identify as Methodist wrestled with the question of whether it was important for their next CEO to be Methodist. Another board wrestled with how important it was for the next CEO to have fundraising experience when less than 10 percent of its revenue base is derived from fundraising. Yet another board engaged in a discussion of how vital it was for the next CEO to have a sophisticated information technology background so the organization could effectively compete with its for-profit competitors.

After these conversations occur, the board—possibly with the help of a consultant—is ready to craft a CEO blueprint that describes what the board is looking for in its next candidate. It also allows internal candidates to privately assess whether they have the appropriate skill sets to be considered. In more sophisticated organizations, it may allow for the organization to provide new responsibilities to a potential internal candidate to assess whether she can fill in current existing gaps on her résumé before the ultimate decision is made.

Understanding the *what* first makes it easier for the board or search firm to actively recruit outside candidates because they know what type of ideal candidate they are looking for. It also prevents a candidate who is uncommonly good at interviewing to wow the board during the interview process even though he doesn't have the exact skill sets the board is looking for. I recently served on an interview committee that was seeking their next leader for a very complex, international organization. Our final two candidates were both talented but couldn't have been more different. One was a candidate who, because of his lack of international experience, would have had a steep learning curve and no obvious mentor to help him along the way. The other possessed significant international and complex organizational experience. Both had the requisite character, integrity, and passion necessary for the role. The first candidate turned out to be an outstanding interviewee, easily engaging and connecting with the interview committee. This led to a couple of board members initially leaning toward this candidate. Because the question of what we were looking for had already been decided, it was easy for the remaining members of the board to remind their colleagues that the first candidate, while a wonderful person, simply didn't have the skill sets we were looking for.

In another situation, two camps had developed within the board. One felt strongly that the internal candidate was the only real right choice, and the other felt just as strongly about the external candidate. Fearing a standoff, the board chair began the board discussion by asking each board member to describe how his or her choice matched up against the organizational blueprint that described what attributes they were looking for in a candidate. This process helped some board members get past the purely emotional reasons they had for their initial preference and, after extensive conversations, the board rallied around the candidate who most closely matched *what* they were looking for as their next CEO.

CHAPTER 38

The Role of the Outgoing CEO

The art of succession planning also requires the board chair, in consultation with the board, to determine what role the outgoing CEO should play in the succession process. Ideally, there is value to including the outgoing CEO as an active participant in many aspects of the succession process.[39]

Part of this, of course, involves why the CEO is departing. If he is being encouraged by the board to retire or move on, there may not be enough trust to bring him into the board's confidence. In this situation, he may need to be managed like other stakeholders. Assuming, however, that there remains a close, trusting relationship between the board and the outgoing CEO, there can be significant value to walking the fine line between including her in the process while at the same time not abrogating the board's responsibility for selecting the next CEO.

A healthy succession-planning process includes trust and a sense of shared purpose between the board and the outgoing CEO, even though their roles will begin to diverge. It is the board's responsibility to select the CEO. This should not be informally delegated to the outgoing CEO; doing so places the outgoing CEO in a difficult position. Often the outgoing CEO has devoted immense energy to preparing an internal candidate and has grown close to that individual. The CEO also sometimes believes that he knows what is best for the organization, as he lives it 24/7, while the board only shows up for quarterly meetings.

The resulting stress also has the potential to get magnified, as the identity of the outgoing CEO is about to change. For years, he has always been identified first as a CEO. In a short time, he will lose this outsized aspect of his identity. This can sometimes cause otherwise good people to make poor decisions. The art of choosing a successor requires the board—and especially the board chair—to overcommunicate with the CEO, to involve the CEO as much as possible when appropriate, and to understand how potentially difficult this is for him and the employees of the organization.

It takes significant emotional maturity for the outgoing CEO to be comfortable moving to a new role and identity. The art of being an outstanding CEO is shown in the ultimate test of your success as a CEO: Does your organization provide an even greater value to society after your tenure? Have you done everything in your power to set the organization up for success? Once a CEO recognizes this and possesses the necessary emotional maturity, she will be able to become a true partner with the board in succession planning. She will make decisions during the last chapter of her tenure to accomplish this goal, including at times intentionally becoming *less* so that the organization and other leaders can become *more*. To quote President Harry Truman, "It is amazing what you can accomplish if you do not care who gets the credit."[40]

The CEO, for example, can play an invaluable role in keeping the internal staff calm and appropriately updating them on the status of the process. The CEO can add considerable value by providing input as to what skill sets are needed in the next CEO as well as reviewing documents for accuracy and improvement. She may know of outside external candidates who should be encouraged to apply. She can provide her assessment as to the readiness of any internal candidate. However, it is generally not appropriate for an outgoing CEO to participate in either the interview or the deliberation process. Having the CEO present may inhibit candidates or the board from being completely open when describing necessary changes for fear of hurting the feelings of the current CEO. At the end of the day, after receiving counsel from the CEO as well as other stakeholders, this decision is the board's and the board's only.

CHAPTER 39

The Qualities of Your Next CEO

The answer to what qualities in an individual an organization should look for when searching for their next CEO goes to the heart of the art of governance. One aspect is, of course, situational— depending on the needs of the organization. Is it a current priority for the next CEO to be a turnaround expert, organizational builder, fundraiser, alliance builder, strategist, industry expert, visionary, or team leader? Is global or complex organizational experience critical? Where does technology expertise fit within the desired skill sets? Most organizations will be able to narrow this type of list to two or three as top priorities.

The world in which every organization operates has gotten more complex, the stakeholders more demanding, the fishbowl ever brighter. In many organizations, CEOs will need to develop the skill set to navigate, or at least manage, the digital arena. Clients, customers, and employees expect their online experience to be as rewarding at your organization as it is with Amazon, Netflix, or Spotify. Those who rely on donors to support their organization can no longer rely simply on a direct-mail and fundraising/events team. Best practices indicate a multipronged approach that includes a targeted social-media strategy, complete with return-on-investment metrics, the purchase and use of big data to effectively identify and target potential donors, and a multitiered strategy that is distinct for each generation. For some organizations, this may demand a six- or seven-figure fundraising investment, which adds substantial pressure on the CEO and her team to get it right.

In today's complex world, organizations are increasingly utilizing data to provide objective analysis for decision-making. This could include a sophisticated tracking of the effectiveness of the organization's compensation philosophy and its impact on retention across employee classes. This could include measuring the effectiveness of how well a client is served via evidence-based and evidence-informed best practices. This could include utilizing a business analyst to better assess the potential return on investment on a new market opportunity. No longer does the CEO have the luxury of managing by her gut. Facts and data matter, and many boards will demand that CEOs have the skill set of managing facts and data going forward.

To meet this seemingly impossible array of challenges, the CEO of today must be a natural lifelong learner. The skill sets that a CEO needs today will not be the same as two or four years from now. My role as CEO significantly evolved at least five times during the past twenty years. To remain successful, I had no choice but to learn and adapt. This is what we have previously described as a *growth mindset*. People who approach leadership roles from this perspective understand that skills and intelligence, like muscle, can be developed. They are more likely to embrace feedback because they know it will ultimately make them better. They perceive hard work as a path to mastery and look forward to being evaluated by the board and their peers.[41]

What boards sometimes underestimate is the influence that a CEO has on the organization's culture. From board members to the direct-care staff of an organization, everyone's skill sets are growing obsolete at a faster and faster rate. Understanding whether a candidate can successfully influence organizational culture by creating an external orientation and a continuous learning environment may also be one of the foci of the selection process. A board that I am involved with recently asked their CEO to resign. While he possessed all the necessary technical skills to be successful, his militaristic management style poisoned the organizational culture and valued employees were choosing to leave, placing the organization at risk.

Finally, it is a given that a leader must be authentic and act with integrity. A leader simply cannot fake being authentic, because ultimately the truth will come out. In addition to having the requisite *what*, a successful CEO will need to possess an abundance of emotional intelligence. Emotional intelligence includes both personal competencies—your ability to be aware of your emotions and appropriately manage your behavior—and social competencies—your ability to be attuned to other people's moods, motives, and behaviors.[42] Most CEO roles require the skill set that the CEO be effective in engaging others. This persuasive art comes naturally to some. However, it is also a skill that can often be intentionally honed through work with a leadership coach. There is an art and a science to successful stakeholder engagement, and a CEO will need to be versed in both.

CHAPTER 40

Every CEO Search
Is Unique

The art of governance matters because there is no blueprint for selecting your organization's next CEO. On one occasion, the outgoing CEO did not have confidence that the board would make the right choice. He had gotten crossways with the board and believed that the board was not capable of being a true partner. He had a favorite internal candidate whom he was sure was the right individual, and he could not understand why the board had hired a search firm to conduct a nationwide search. The role of the board chair was simply to manage the outgoing CEO during the process so that he didn't cause harm to the organization. This situation also required the board chair to reach out to other members of the senior leadership team to assure them that the board had created an appropriate process so they could have confidence that the board would make a good decision. The board fulfilled its fiduciary responsibility and interviewed numerous candidates. The board unanimously selected the best candidate, which happened to be the internal candidate preferred by the CEO. The result was that, through dialogue and action, members of the senior leadership team, including the newly selected CEO, had a renewed respect for the board, which allowed it to repair the previously strained relationship and move forward.

Earlier, I alluded to the fact that we got right five of the six search processes that I have played a leadership role in. While accurate, we also came close in another search to making a damaging decision. In both situations—the one where we failed and the other where we nearly failed—the search committee felt pressure because the organizations at the time were financially teetering. Both called for changes in management due to the rapidly changing external environment in which the organizations operated. What worked in the past was simply not going to be successful going forward.

In the first situation, there was a need to quickly create new revenue streams. We interviewed a divisional vice president of a similar organization who had an amazing track record of growth in his division, which was a product area our organization was weak in. He promised that he could produce similar results by selling a similar product for our organization, which would, in turn, solve the financial woes of the entire organization. The search committee became so enamored by the idea of a quick fix that we failed to assess whether the candidate had the requisite emotional intelligence and skill sets to manage the entire universe of stakeholders, as he would assume a position two levels above his current position. The promised results never materialized, and it quickly became apparent that this individual was in over his head. It was a classic example of how "savior" candidates often don't work. Five years later, the board and he agreed that it would be in everyone's best interest if he retired. While the organization was able to stay afloat, they were no better off because of his tenure.

In a second similar situation, an even more potentially damaging mistake almost was made. We were down to the last few candidates. We knew that there were no quick fixes, and we were looking for a candidate who could bring the stakeholders together, craft a strategic plan, create new revenue streams to replace the old, and then work tirelessly to execute the plan. Our search committee came close to losing our compass as we temporarily drifted from having clarity on what we were looking for and instead became enamored with an outsized personality who was able to work the room with ease and came with a rags-to-riches story. Because of his charisma, we took him at his word when he answered our questions about a couple of minor holes in his résumé. Fortunately, the committee came back to its senses and chose the individual that fit closest to what we were looking for, including a track record of producing results. Not too long after, the individual that we did not choose was hired as CEO of a similar organization. A few months later, he was no longer there due to ethical mishaps. This experience is a reminder to all boards of the importance of vetting candidates. A nonnegotiable aspect of the interview process is to thoroughly investigate the character of each candidate.

The act of selecting the right CEO will always be part art and part science. The goal of every organization should be to create a process that allows the board to interview potential candidates in a manner that reduces the risk of selecting the wrong candidate. Not only is this the most important decision a board will be tasked with, but it also has the most risk. The goal of the process is to reduce this risk. Fortunately, there are several available levers to pull to reduce the risk of getting a decision wrong.

One is to observe the candidate in different settings. Take her out to dinner. Include her spouse. Watch the candidate give a presentation. How candidates act in social settings can speak volumes about their ability to be effective CEOs. Several board members and I once had dinner with a prospective candidate and his spouse. We were dismayed at how poorly he treated his wife during the dinner; this led us to notice other potential character lapses in this individual. Another had trouble keeping a social conversation going during a breakfast, which provided us an indication of his emotional intelligence.

It is helpful to have a couple of board members involved in the search process whose professional experience matches this type of organization. They may be able to drill down deeper during the interview process to truly assess whether the candidate meets the *what* the board is seeking. It may be appropriate to ask a former board member to be a member of the search committee if that individual has a valued organizational-related skill set that the current board may not have.

One not inconsequential benefit of creating a healthy and effective board governance framework is that it can be used as a recruiting tool to attract best-in-class candidates. There have been several potential professional opportunities that I quickly removed my name from consideration in large part because I learned through the grapevine how convoluted or dysfunctional their board-governance system was. Alternatively, many current CEOs would readily trade their current board-governance experience and make a lateral move if they were assured that they would be working with an emotionally intelligent, ethical, adaptive, carefully selected, competency-based board of directors that possessed a passion for the mission. Good board governance matters when recruiting and retaining outstanding CEOs.

CHAPTER 41

The Art of Measuring and Compensating the CEO for Success

There is both a science and an art to utilizing compensation and benefits for the CEO and leadership team to further the mission of the organization. The science, of course, is making sure that your practices are ethical and not in violation of IRS rules governing nonprofit organizations. It is understanding your organization's compensation philosophy and knowing where to find comparative data as to what other similar organizations are paying their executives. Salary surveys of nonprofit organizations that provide compensation ranges for various positions broken down by region and size of the organization are useful as a starting point. It is also understanding the financial realities of what is available in the compensation pool based on your organization's financial situation and size.

The art of compensating a CEO has become more complex in recent years, but it can become a competitive advantage if done properly. In the nonprofit world, it is a given today that employees, funders, and stakeholders have access to the details of your executives' annual compensation, as it is readily available on the internet-accessible IRS 990 forms. As many nonprofit organizations are increasingly looking to the for-profit world to recruit leaders who possess both a sense of mission and complex organization experience, this too may impact the terms of the agreement. Boards must continually balance the potential appearance of overcompensating their executives with the need to recruit and retain the most qualified people.

One question best-in-class organizations wrestle with is, What is the organization's compensation philosophy? For example, one organization strives to pay each employee at the 50th percentile salary level and the 75th percentile in terms of overall benefits. The organization also believes that outstanding senior leadership is a differentiator. So for top executives, the board and staff established a compensation philosophy at the 75th percentile for both salary and benefits.

Recently, a personnel committee realized that the various pools they had recruited their four top executives from all had unique compensation characteristics. One set of data simply didn't fit each unique situation. For example, the pool that they recruited their CEO from included university presidents, the political arena, and large national nonprofit organizations. The pool that they recruited their CFO from was comprised of large non-profit organizations, Big Four accounting firms, and for-profit organizations of similar complexity. The pool to recruit and retain the Chief External Relations Officer was large national nonprofit organizations. They were also aware that their highly talented COO was being actively recruited by both large nonprofit and for-profit organizations. While they knew they could never match the for-profit world in terms of potential compensation, they worked hard at creating a package that would be appealing to her. The personnel committee correctly decided that they needed to work with an outside consulting firm to help navigate the complexities of these various situations, with the goal being to create a fair and attractive compensation package for all four individuals that would further the mission of the organization and continue to meet the guidelines of IRS requirements as they relate to nonprofit executives.

The art of compensation dictates that you assess the market and have an honest conversation with the CEO about what is important to him. It may be financial security, flexibility of schedule, benefits, the ability to occasionally work remotely, the creation of a rabbi trust, or a 457(b) retirement plan. It may be the opportunity to continue to develop his skill sets. Assuming you have the right CEO, the question becomes how to retain him. Again, this is like a marriage; both sides must actively engage in a grace-filled, open dialogue to create a successful, long-lasting partnership.

In one situation, the board had successfully recruited a high-profile star as their next CEO, and they wanted to make sure that this individual would not be recruited away during the next few years to a larger organization. They crafted an agreement that included a retention clause that provided a certain amount of additional money in a lump-sum payment at the end of each calendar year, with the handcuff being that if the CEO voluntarily left the organization before the end of the contract, he would be responsible for paying back to the organization the compensation he received under the terms of the retention bonus.

In another situation, the incoming CEO was worried about the soundness of her retirement situation. Options that the board discussed with the CEO included utilizing various levers such as a rabbi trust, a 457(b) plan, and/or an annual lump-sum retirement bonus that would have to be reimbursed back to the organization if the CEO stayed fewer than five years. The value of engaging in such discussions is that the board understands what is and is not important to the incoming CEO and can then craft a package where the CEO no longer needs to worry about her financial future and can focus instead on the mission of the organization.

Here is an example of what can occur when there is complete trust between a board and a CEO: As board chair, I was tasked with having the initial conversation with the newly selected CEO. When I mentioned that we needed to have a conversation about his compensation package, his response was, "Whatever you offer me I will accept because I trust you and the board, and I know that you will have done your homework and it will be fair." This may have been the nicest governance compliment I have ever received. It was an indication that we had handled the search process transparently and fairly. It also placed great pressure on the board to ensure that we did live up to the CEO's expectations.

Another newly selected CEO almost didn't accept the job because the board did not pay enough attention to him after they had selected him. When he flew in from out of town to talk about the employment offer, no one met him at the airport. Neither had they arranged to take him to dinner. The next morning, when he met with the board chair, it was clear that this was the board chair's first time negotiating an employment agreement. He didn't know what to do other than offer the CEO the same agreement that the previous CEO had received. The incoming CEO came away with the impression that the board was unengaged and less than competent. He felt deflated from the lack of attention he was receiving as he was about to accept his first role as CEO.

Fortunately, the board chair and CEO had developed a relationship with the search process consultant and separately called him to share their frustrations. The consultant was able to educate the board chair as to the importance of building a relationship with the CEO and that several new terms to the contract should possibly be considered to meet the unique needs of the CEO's situation. Both returned to the table and came to a meeting of the minds. Over a decade later, this CEO remains with the organization and has led the organization to levels previously not imaginable.

CHAPTER 42

Determining CEO-Board Success

How will the CEO and the board know if they have successfully embraced the art of governance? By how they honestly answer the following questions:

- Is there a healthy, trusting relationship between the CEO and the board where both parties believe they are effectively using their talents and working in concert toward a common, well-defined vision and mission?

- Is the CEO comfortable sharing everything with the board? Or does he selectively share information as part of his agenda to manage the board?

- Are the board and the CEO spending at least half of their time together looking strategically into the future?

- Have the elephants in the room been identified and wrestled with in a blame-free, trust-filled environment?

- Does the board have the requisite collective skill sets? is it appropriately diverse?

- Do the board and the CEO regularly engage in the topic of succession planning?

- Are there appropriate checks and balances in place where both the board and the CEO are clear about their respective roles and hold each other accountable?

- Can both the board and the CEO clearly articulate an agreed-upon focused strategy that is being effectively implemented and appropriately measured?

- Does the CEO believe that she is being supported by the board and does the board feel supported by the CEO?

In my experience, even the healthiest board-CEO partnership will discover low-hanging fruit to improve on. This is simply the nature of any relationship. This is especially true within board dynamics as various participants come and go, the external environment evolves, and new opportunities and challenges arise. It is the healthiest of boards and CEOs that are often the hardest in terms of assessing themselves, driven to be the very best that they can be. I remain convinced that this shared journey is worth the effort as the participants will increasingly discover that their intentional, healthy, shared partnership is indeed a competitive advantage.

CHAPTER 43

Bringing Our Entire Being to the Table

Given how difficult the role of being a board member or CEO has become, the question arises, Why would anyone voluntarily assume such a responsibility? While I can't speak for others, I can share why such service is important to me.

As a Christian, I am privileged to view my service to the community from a unique lens. I am secure in my belief that my life isn't just some random event. Rather, I was envisioned by my Father in heaven long before I was born here on earth:

- For I know the plans I have for you, declares the LORD, plans for welfare and not for evil, to give you a future and a hope. (Jeremiah 29:11)

- For we are His workmanship, created in Christ Jesus for good works, which God prepared beforehand, that we should walk in them. (Ephesians 2:10)

God, in His infinite wisdom, gave each of us different gifts. The apostle Paul writes, "Having gifts that differ according to the grace given to us, let us use them: if prophecy, in proportion to our faith; if service, in our serving; the one who teaches, in his teaching; the one who exhorts, in his exhortation; the one who contributes, in generosity; the one who leads, with zeal; the one who does acts of mercy, with cheerfulness" (Romans 12:6–8). And, as Christ instructs in the parable of the talents, we are to use and grow our gifts from God for His glory (see Matthew 25:14–30).

As I prayerfully discern how I am to be of service to my neighbor, God speaks to me through my Baptism, daily reading of His Word, worship, and the Lord's Table, enabling me to discern the calling that is uniquely mine. And as I prayerfully ponder my calling, I see more clearly that He has graciously endowed me with certain gifts that can serve to strengthen organizations, enabling them to be more impactful in achieving their mission. The same is true for you. Not only has God given each of you a unique set of talents, passions, and skills, but He has also providentially placed you in a unique opportunity to serve your organization.[43]

God's Word offers great insight that instructs us in our shared governance vocation and missional journey. It might even be said that the Bible provides the insight necessary to embrace the art of governance.

And let us not grow weary of doing good, for in due season we will reap, if we do not give up. (Galatians 6:9)

Iron sharpens iron, and one man sharpens another. (Proverbs 27:17)

Do nothing from selfish ambition or conceit, but in humility count others more significant than yourselves. (Philippians 2:3)

Know well the condition of your flocks, and give attention to your herds, for riches do not last forever; and does a crown endure to all generations? (Proverbs 27:23–24)

So whatever you wish that others would do to you, do also to them, for this is the Law and the Prophets. (Matthew 7:12)

Behold, I am sending you out as sheep in the midst of wolves, so be wise as serpents and innocent as doves. (Matthew 10:16)

Viewed from this lens, when we step into a boardroom, participate in a Zoom board call, counsel a CEO, or create a shared partnership with the board, our only purpose is to come together to accomplish our shared mission—or dare I say, *His* mission—knowing that collectively we can utilize our God-given talents to harness a greater impact than we could by ourselves. We must become less as our shared work is bigger and more important than any of us. It is an opportunity to positively impact the lives of our clients, community, and employees, to be the hands and feet of Christ here on this earth.

Conclusion

As a board member, you are given an almost impossible responsibility. You are asked, on a part-time, often unpaid basis, to oversee an increasingly complex organization. Employees, clients, customers, vendors, donors, stakeholders, and the community at large depend on you to get this right. As a CEO, you are charged both with fulfilling your role of moving the organization forward while also creating an environment so that the board, working as a partner with you, is positioned to support, oversee, and add value to the organization. Both the CEO and the board are tasked with intentionally creating a framework of governance that ensures that the organization will continue to thrive well into the future.

What CEOs crave is to work with a board that adds value to the organization, that truly is a strategic partner. What boards crave is the ability to leverage their time and knowledge to enhance the organization and support the CEO. It is in the power of both the CEO and the board to make this happen. For an organization's governance approach to become a competitive advantage will take creativity, intentionality, honest dialogue, trust, and the ability to adapt as the external and internal environments evolve and players continually change. By redesigning how and what information is shared, and by creating tailored opportunities for the board to add strategic value to the organization, the CEO and the board will be able to walk in lockstep toward achieving their shared vision and mission.

This is the art of governance. Is this shared journey worth the effort? From my perspective, we simply have no choice. If we want our schools, hospitals, museums, universities, trade associations, faith-based organizations, foundations, social-service organizations, and churches to add value to our communities and the world in which we live, it is imperative for us to artfully create a board-governance structure that becomes a competitive advantage.

It is my prayer that you, as a board member and senior leader, will embrace this solemn responsibility. Your clients, members, customers, employees, and communities that you serve depend on you. The world depends on you. I close with wisdom from the apostle Paul:

Therefore, since we are surrounded by so great a cloud of witnesses, let us also lay aside every weight, and sin which clings so closely, and let us run with endurance the race that is set before us, looking to Jesus, the founder and perfector of our faith, . . . so that you may not grow weary or fainthearted. (Hebrews 12:1–3)

Endnotes

1   To learn more about Level 5 leadership traits, see Jim Collins, "Level 5 Leadership: The Triumph of Humility and Fierce Resolve," *Harvard Business Review*, January 1, 2001, hrb.org/2001/01/level-5-leadership-the-triumph-of-humility-and-fierce-resolve-2

2   Sarbanes-Oxley Act of 2002, Public Law 107–204, 107th Congress, enacted July 30, 2002 (the "Sarbanes-Oxley Act"), available at http://findlaw.com/hdocs/docs/gwbush/sarbanesoxley072302.pdf.

3   John Carver, *Boards That Make a Difference: A New Design for Leadership in Nonprofit and Public Organizations*, third ed. (San Francisco: Jossey Bass, 2006).

4   See, for example, "Governance Issues," ESG | The Report (website), www.esgthereport.com/what-is-esg/the-g-in-esg/what-is-corporate-governance/governance-issues/.

5   Mark Twain, *Following the Equator: A Journey Around the World* (Hartford: American Publishing Co., 1897), ch. 61.

6   Peter F. Drucker, *Management: Tasks, Responsibilities, Practices* (New York: Harper Collins, 1974), 628.

7   John Carver and Miriam Carver, "Carver's Policy Governance Model in Nonprofit Organizations," Policy Governance®, www.carvergovernance.com/pg-np.htm.

8   Richard P. Chait, Barbara E. Taylor, and William P. Ryan, *Governance as Leadership: Reframing the Work of Nonprofit Boards* (Hoboken: Wiley, 2005).

9   Colin B. Carter and Jay W. Lorsch, *Back to the Drawing Board: Designing Corporate Boards for a Complex World* (Boston: Harvard Business School Press, 2004).

10 Carver, *Boards That Make a Difference.*

11 In the nonprofit world, C-suite refers to the group of high-ranking executives within the organization. Typically, but not always, it refers to the group of people who report to the CEO.

12 "Recommended Board Practices," BoardSource (website), accessed on November 14, 2022, https://boardsource.org/recommended-board-practices.

13 Daniel Goleman, *Emotional Intelligence: Why It Can Matter More Than IQ* (New York: Bantam Books, 1995).

14 Goleman, *Emotional Intelligence*, 142–45.

15 Goleman, *Emotional Intelligence*, 145.

16 See, for example, Justin Menkes, *Executive Intelligence: What All Great Leaders Have* (New York: Harper Collins, 2009).

17 Carter, *Back to the Drawing Board*, 64–83.

18 For further insight, see "Boards Roles and Responsibilities," National Council of Nonprofits, https://www.councilofnonprofits.org/tools-resources/board-roles-and-responsibilities .

19 Jim Taylor, "The Four Principles of Purpose-Driven Board Leadership," Board-Source (website), Presentation at Lutheran Services in America-CEO Summit, January 26, 2022.

20 Vivian Hunt, Dennis Layton, and Sara Prince, *Why Diversity Matters* (McKinsey and Company, January 2015). See also *Diversity Wins: How Inclusion Matters* (McKinsey and Company, May 2020).

21 Amy Picchi, "Goldman Sachs' New IPO Rule: No More All-White, Male Boards," *Money Watch*, January 24, 2020.

22 David F. Larcker, Nicholas E. Donatiello, Bill Meehan, and Brian Tayan, "2015 Survey on Board of Directors of Nonprofit Organizations," Stanford Graduate School of Business, https://www.gsb.stanford.edu/faculty-research/publications/2015-survey-board-directors-nonprofit-organizations.

23 For a more detailed analysis, see "Can Board Members Be Paid?" National Council of Nonprofits, https://www.councilofnonprofits.org/tools-resources/can-board-members-be-paid.

24 Taylor Defoe, "Want to Hear a Radical Nonprofit Strategy? After Laying Off Its Full-Time Staff, A Blade of Grass Will Now Pay Its Board Members," Artnet, https://news.artnet.com/about/taylor-dafoe-731, March 17, 2022.

25 See, for example, Carter, *Back to the Drawing Board*, 86–91.

26 Carol Dweck, *Mindset: The New Psychology of Success* (New York: Random House, 2006).

27 Goleman, *Emotional Intelligence*, 142.

28 Goleman, *Emotional Intelligence*, 143–45.

29 *The Mach 1 Group Newsletter*, April 2022, Issue 27, p. 1.

30 Jim Collins, *Good to Great: Why Some Companies Make the Leap and Others Don't* (New York: Harper Business, 2001).

31 Jim Collins, *Good to Great and the Social Sectors: Why Business Thinking Is Not the Answer* (New York: Harper Collins, 2011).

32 For an in-depth examination of how to implement this type of strategic framework, see Rupert Younger, Colin Mayer, and Robert G. Eccles, *Enacting Purpose within the Modern Corporation: A Framework for Boards of Directors* (University of Oxford, Said Business School, 2020), https://www.enactingpurpose.org/assets/enacting-purpose-initiative---eu-report-august-2020.pdf.

33 For a deeper discussion on the organizational benefits of following the golden rule,

see Kurt Senske, *Executive Values: A Christian Approach to Organizational Leadership* (Minneapolis: Augsburg Books, 2003).

34 For an excellent resource, see, Henry Cloud, *Necessary Endings: The Employees, Businesses, and Relationships That All of Us Have to Give Up in Order to Move Forward* (New York: Harper Collins, 2010).

35 Cloud, *Necessary Endings*, 199–210.

36 Patrick M. Wright, Donald J. Schlepker, Anthony J. Nyberg, and Michael D. Ulrich, *CEO Succession Success: A Board Perspective*, Center for Executive Succession, University of South Carolina, https://sc.edu/study/colleges_schools/moore/documents/center_for_executive_succession/ceo_succession_success.pdf.

37 Jim Schleckser, "Should a Board Consider an Insider or an Outsider for a CEO Succession?" Inc. (website), https://www.inc.com/jim-schleckser/should-a-board-consider-an-insider-or-an-outsider-for-a-ceo-succession.html.

38 For further insight, see, Ram Charan, "The Secrets of Great CEO Selection," *Harvard Business Review*, https://hbr.org/2016/12/the-secrets-of-great-ceo-selection.

39 *Nominating/Governance Committee: Succession Planning*, Spencer Stuart, https://www.spencerstuart.com/-/media/2020/february/nomgov_successionplanning_feb2020.pdf

40 Harry S. Truman, quotation from Truman Library Institute (website), https://www.trumanlibraryinstitute.org/truman/truman-quotes/page/5/.

41 Dweck, *Mindset*.

42 Travis Bradberry and Jean Greaves, *Emotional Intelligence 2.0* (San Diego: Talent Smart, 2009), 23–24.

43 For further insight on how to live the life that God created uniquely for you, see Kurt Senske, *The Calling: Live a Life of Significance* (St. Louis: Concordia Publishing House, 2010).

About the Author

Dr. Kurt Senske is the founder and principal of CEO-Board Services, a consulting firm that specializes in working with mission-oriented organizational leaders and boards around issues of governance, strategy, organizational structure, succession planning, coaching, and mergers and acquisitions.

For twenty-three years, Dr. Senske served as CEO of Upbring (formerly Lutheran Social Services of the South), a multi-faceted, multi-state social service agency with an annual operating budget of more than $100 million and 1,000 employees. At Upbring, Dr. Senske more than quadrupled the size of the agency and steered the once-troubled agency back to financial strength. During his tenure, the organization eliminated an indebtedness of $60 million and currently enjoys an endowment of more than $40 million.

Dr. Senske completed his undergraduate work at Concordia University Texas and Valparaiso University, majoring in accounting, with a bachelor of science degree in business administration. He holds a Juris Doctor from the University of Illinois College of Law, a master of arts degree in international relations from Schiller International University in Paris, France, and a PhD in government from the University of Texas at Austin.

Prior to his work at Upbring, Dr. Senske served as the assistant to the president at Concordia University Texas. Dr. Senske also practiced law in Chicago, Illinois, with several law firms, including Hinshaw and Culbertson. In addition, he has served as a senior staff member and policy adviser for government leaders at local, state, and national levels for both the Republican and Democratic parties.

Dr. Senske's extensive board service includes having served as chair of the board of directors of Thrivent Financial, a Fortune 500 financial services organization. He currently serves as chair of Thrivent Charitable and as chair of Lutheran Hour Ministries.

Dr. Senske is the author of five books, including *Wine and the Word: Savor and Serve*; *The Calling: Live a Life of Significance*; and *Executive Values: A Christian Approach to Organizational Leadership.*

A gifted public speaker, Dr. Senske has also been a guest columnist on a variety of issues for newspapers and magazines as well as a regular commentator on television and radio. He and his wife, Laurie, live in Austin, Texas, along with their daughter, Sydney, and son-in-law, Cody.

Dr. Senske can be reached at kurtsenske@gmail.com.